Better Homes and Gardens®

PRESSURE COOKER

COOKBOOK

BETTER HOMES AND GARDENS® BOOKS
Des Moines

BETTER HOMES AND GARDENS® BOOKS
An Imprint of Meredith® Books

PRESSURE COOKER COOKBOOK
Editor: Lisa Mannes
Contributing Editors: Joanne Fullan and Pat Ward
Associate Art Director: Tom Wegner
Test Kitchen Product Supervisors: Diana Nolin and
  Colleen Weeden
Food Stylist: Janet Pittman
Photographer: Mike Dieter
Electronic Production Coordinator: Paula Forest
Production Manager: Douglas Johnston

Vice President and Editorial Director: Elizabeth P. Rice
Executive Editor: Kay M. Sanders
Art Director: Ernest Shelton
Managing Editor: Christopher Cavanaugh
Test Kitchen Director: Sharon Stilwell

President, Book Group: Joseph J. Ward
Vice President, Retail Marketing: Jamie L. Martin
Vice President, Direct Marketing: Timothy Jarrell

On the cover: Garlic Chicken (see recipe, page 39)

Meredith Corporation
Chairman of the Executive Committee: E.T. Meredith III
Chairman of the Board and Chief Executive Officer:
Jack D. Rehm
President and Chief Operating Officer: William T. Kerr

WE CARE!

All of us at Better Homes and Gardens® Books are
dedicated to providing you with the information and ideas
you need to create delicious food. We welcome your
questions, comments, or suggestions. Please write to us at:
Better Homes and Gardens Books, Editorial Dept.,
LN-112, 1716 Locust Street, Des Moines, IA 50309-3023.

Our seal assures you that every recipe in *Pressure Cooker
Cookbook* has been tested in the Better Homes and
Gardens® Test Kitchen. This means that each recipe is
practical and reliable, and meets our highest standards of
taste appeal. We guarantee your satisfaction with this book
for as long as you own it.

INTRODUCTION

Pressure cooker sales are on the rise, and with good reason. Health-conscious American cooks like you want good food but they don't want to spend hours and hours cooking it. So, many are turning to the pressure cooker—a reliable way to produce healthy, low-fat dishes in no time.

Americans first learned of the pressure cooker in 1939, when it was introduced by National Presto Industries at the World's Fair. American cooks embraced this European invention and used it to turn out meals in record time. Later, with the advent of fast-food restaurants and frozen TV dinners, cooks found other quick ways to feed their families.

Today, Americans are increasingly bored with fast-food restaurants and disappointed with the quality of frozen convenience foods. They want the comfort foods of the '50s, but with the sophisticated flavors and speed of the '90s. The pressure cooker helps achieve those objectives. There are more than 20 brands of domestic and imported pressure cookers on the market, in a wide range of prices. These pressure cookers are safer than ever, designed with one or more mechanisms that prevent the buildup of excess pressure.

In this book, you'll discover 90 flavorful recipes that cook to perfection in minutes in the pressure cooker. As a result, these recipes take pressure off you.

CONTENTS

Pressure Cooker Basics —————————— 6

Discover how pressure cookers work. Learn about the
two kinds of cookers and their safety features. This chapter also
offers cooking tips, cooking directions, and suggestions for
adapting your favorite recipes to this timesaving device.

Soups, Stews, Chilies, and Chowders ——— 12

Choose from an abundance of robust soups and stews with
long-simmered flavor and short cooking times. You'll also
find a treasury of chilies and chowders sure to please. Every
recipe in this chapter can serve as a main dish—just add a
crusty loaf of bread and a green salad.

Poultry and Meat ————————————— 38

This chapter brims with comfort food for the '90s. We've
updated family favorites such as barbecued ribs, pot roast with
vegetables, and stuffed pork chops. Try new dishes too,
such as Pheasant in Port Wine, Thai Beef and Broccoli, and
Warm Chicken Salad.

Vegetarian Main Dishes _____ 61

Discover a wide array of protein-rich main dishes. Many rely on dried beans—navy, pinto, black, and garbanzo. For each recipe, we include information on soaking the beans. You will also get acquainted with grains such as couscous and quinoa. Other sensational dishes are served over rice.

Vegetable Side Dishes _____ 72

Once you pressure-cook winter vegetables, you'll wonder why you didn't use this appliance sooner. The variety of recipes in this chapter will inspire you to consider these vegetables as more than side dishes.

Desserts _____ 86

Surprisingly, many old-fashioned desserts cook beautifully and quickly under pressure. Try the creamy, rich Caramel Custard or individual-sized Cinnamon Ricotta Cheesecakes. For chocolate lovers, there's a fabulous Creamy Chocolate Cheesecake. Don't forget the bread puddings—there are four to try.

HOW PRESSURE COOKERS WORK

It seems almost magical the first few times you cook with a pressure cooker. Foods that usually take hours to cook are done to perfection in one-third the usual cooking time. The principle of cooking under pressure is quite simple. After the lid is locked, the liquid in the cooker starts boiling and produces steam. The trapped steam causes pressure to build and the temperature in the cooker actually rises above the boiling point.

Let's backtrack a little. At sea level, the atmospheric pressure is 14.7 pounds per square inch and the boiling point of water is 212 degrees Fahrenheit. Inside the cooker, pressure increases to 15 pounds per square inch and the boiling point increases to 250 degrees Fahrenheit.

Because of the higher boiling temperature and the additional steam, pressure-cooked foods cook more quickly than normal. The steam softens the food fibers so that tough meats and fibrous vegetables become tender in minutes. The flavors of combined ingredients in the resulting dishes seem more intense.

TYPES OF PRESSURE COOKERS

There are two basic types of pressure cookers: first- and second-generation cookers. A first-generation pressure cooker has a removable pressure regulator that is either a single-control or a selective-control regulator. With a single-control cooker, all foods are cooked at 15 pounds pressure. When cooking pressure is reached, the pressure regulator rocks gently and makes a hissing sound. If you have a selective-control cooker, you can cook at 5, 10, or 15 pounds pressure. For this book, you need only use 15 pounds pressure. When this cooker reaches 15 pounds pressure, the regulator begins to rock or jiggle. When movement begins, reduce the heat just enough to maintain the rocking.

Second-generation pressure cookers have stationary pressure regulators. They use an indicator rod to show when pressure is reached and they make little or no noise. You watch the indicator and when pressure is reached reduce the heat, just enough to maintain the desired level.

No matter which pressure cooker you have, be sure to read the manufacturer's instructions before using.

TODAY'S PRESSURE COOKERS ARE SAFE

All pressure cookers are safe to use, but it's important to read the manufacturer's use and care booklet for specific instructions. All cookers have these safety features:

■ The lid must be locked securely in place before the pressure will rise. See your manufacturer's booklet for directions on how to lock the lid.

■ A rubber gasket in the lid prevents opening the cooker until the pressure has been reduced enough to open it safely.

■ Overpressure and/or backup plugs release steam if you forget to reduce the heat under the cooker when 15 pounds pressure is reached or if the vent becomes clogged with food.

PRESSURE COOKER TIPS

All of the recipes in this cookbook have been tested and approved in the Better Homes and Gardens® Test Kitchen. It is important to follow directions carefully for best results.

1. Fill the pressure cooker no more than two-thirds full.

The pressure regulator on the vent pipe maintains the cooking pressure at a safe level. It releases extra pressure during cooking. As a backup, pressure cookers have a secondary pressure plug that is designed to relieve excess pressure if the pressure regulator is not functioning properly. Neither can do its job if clogged with food. Foods tend to expand when cooked under pressure. If the cooker is filled more than two-thirds full, food may block the vent pipe or the backup plug.

If cooking meat, poultry, or bones for stock, be sure that no pieces extend above the two-thirds full level. If cooking soups and stews, the maximum liquid capacity is 10 cups in a 4-quart pressure cooker and 16 cups in a 6-quart cooker.

2. Some foods can't be cooked in a pressure cooker.

Some foods foam during cooking and can clog the vent pipe and backup plug. For safety purposes, we don't recommend cooking the following under pressure: pasta, rice, applesauce, oatmeal or other cereals, split peas, pearl barley, cranberries, or rhubarb.

3. Always make sure the vent pipe is clear.

Hold the lid to the light and look through the vent pipe to be sure it's clear. If it is blocked, use a wire or a wooden toothpick to clean it. If the vent pipe is clogged, pressure may build to unsafe levels.

4. Never open the cooker when it is under pressure.

Always check the indicator or gently push the pressure regulator and listen for noise before attempting to open the pressure cooker.

When pressure is reduced, the lid will open easily. If there is resistance, there may be pressure remaining in the cooker. Wait a few minutes or quick-release pressure by placing cooker in the sink and running cold water down one side of the lid. (If you have a second-generation cooker, you also can quick-release by pressing a button or moving a lever. (See How to Use These Recipes, number 7 on page 10.)

5. Replace the rubber gasket if it becomes hard or soft and sticky.

The sealing gasket usually does not get soft and sticky. However, if the ring often comes in contact with oil or fat, it may soften. It should be replaced to prevent any damage.

6. Never hit a spoon, potato masher, or other utensil on the rim of the cooker.

A small dent in the rim may prevent the cooker from pressurizing properly.

HOW TO USE THESE RECIPES

Because using a pressure cooker may be new to you, here are explanations of cooking directions used in these recipes.

1. In a 4- or 6-quart pressure cooker combine ingredients.

Most of the recipes in this book can be prepared in either a 4-quart or a 6-quart pressure cooker. The stock recipes are exceptions: A 6-quart cooker is needed.

2. Place rack in cooker.

Most cookers come with a rack. If yours did not, use a small wire cooling rack instead. The rack holds the food above the liquid during cooking. New pressure cookers come with steaming baskets which are terrific for cooking vegetables.

3. Lock lid in place.

Refer to your manufacturer's instructions for the correct way to lock your pressure cooker. The cooker must be closed properly for pressure to be reached.

4. Place pressure regulator on vent pipe.

All first-generation pressure cookers have a removable pressure regulator. A single-control regulator cooks only at 15 pounds pressure. A selective-control regulator can cook at 5, 10, and 15 pounds pressure. Select 15 pounds pressure for all the recipes in this book. If you have a second-generation cooker with a stationary pressure regulator, ignore this step.

5. Cook with the pressure regulator rocking gently.

On single-control pressure cookers, the regulator rocks gently when pressure is reached. The regulator jiggles on selective-control cookers. Second-generation cookers include an indicator that tells the pressure. When the regulator shows that

15 pounds pressure is reached, reduce the heat to maintain pressure. Time the recommended length of cooking from this point.

6. Allow pressure to decrease naturally.

Turn off the heat and let cooker stand until no more pressure remains. The food continues to cook as the pressure drops. It may take a few minutes or as long as 20 minutes.

7. Quick-release the pressure.

Place the cooker beneath cold running water until no more pressure remains. Second-generation cookers let you quick-release pressure by moving a lever or pressing a button. Steam will accompany the pressure release.

8. Carefully remove lid.

Turn the handle until the lid releases. Carefully remove the lid, tilting it away from you in case any steam remains inside the cooker.

USING FOIL HANDLES

Some of the recipes in this book use a 1½-quart soufflé dish. With foil handles you easily can lift the dish in and out of the pressure cooker. Here's how to make foil handles:

1. Tear off two 20x2-inch pieces of heavy foil. Crisscross the strips and place a greased 1½-quart soufflé dish in the center.

2. Lift the ends of the foil strips and transfer dish into the cooker. Fold the ends of the foil strips over the top of the dish.

3. Use the foil strips to carefully remove the dish from the cooker.

HOW TO ADAPT YOUR RECIPES

Range-top recipes can be adapted for a pressure cooker if most of the ingredients are put into the cooker at the start. Because the success of cooking under pressure relies on the correct amount of liquid, check the recipes in this book for proportions. For example, if you're making a favorite soup or stew, find a similar recipe in this book and use it to measure the amount of liquid you need and the approximate cooking time.

NUTRITION FACTS

Cooking under pressure generally requires less fat than other cooking methods. Also, pressure-cooked foods are so flavorful they require less salt. We have included nutritional facts per serving for each recipe in this book. The nutritional facts per serving measures calories, total fat, saturated fat, cholesterol, sodium, carbohydrate, fiber, and protein. The percentage of daily value is listed for vitamin A, vitamin C, calcium, and iron. When a recipe gives an ingredient substitution, we used the first choice in the nutritional analysis. If the recipe makes a range of servings (such as 4 to 6), we calculated nutrition information with the smaller number. Optional ingredients aren't included in the calculations.

MINESTRONE

*Pressure cooking intensifies the flavors in this traditional Italian soup
and reduces the cooking time substantially.*

PREPARATION TIME: SOAKING TIME FOR
BEANS PLUS 20 MINUTES
COOKING TIME: 19 MINUTES

- 1 **cup dry great northern
  or cannellini beans**
- 1 **cup coarsely chopped
  onion**
- 1 **cup fresh or loose-pack
  frozen cut green beans**
- 2 **cloves garlic, minced**
- 1 **cup carrots, cut into
  ¼-inch slices
  (2 medium)**
- 1 **teaspoon dried basil,
  crushed**
- 1 **teaspoon dried oregano,
  crushed**
- 2 **14½-ounce cans
  vegetable or beef broth**
- 1 **16-ounce can whole
  Italian-style tomatoes,
  cut up**
- 2 **tablespoons cooking oil**
- 1⅓ **cups zucchini, halved
  lengthwise and cut into
  ½-inch slices
  (1 medium)**
- 1 **cup chopped savoy or
  green cabbage**
- ½ **cup small shell macaroni
  Grated Parmesan cheese
  (optional)**

1. Rinse beans. In a large saucepan combine beans and enough water to cover them. Bring to boiling; reduce heat. Simmer for 2 minutes. Remove from heat. Cover and let stand 1 hour. (Or, omit boiling and soak beans overnight.)

2. Drain and rinse the beans. In a 4- or 6-quart pressure cooker combine beans, onion, fresh green beans (if using), garlic, carrots, basil, oregano, vegetable or beef broth, *undrained* tomatoes, and oil.

3. Lock lid in place. Place pressure regulator on vent pipe (if you have a first-generation cooker). Over high heat, bring cooker up to pressure. Reduce heat just enough to maintain pressure and pressure regulator rocks gently; cook for 12 minutes.

4. Quick-release the pressure. Carefully remove lid.

5. Add frozen green beans (if using), zucchini, cabbage, and macaroni to cooker. Bring to boiling; reduce heat. Cover loosely (do not lock lid) and cook about 5 minutes or till vegetables and macaroni are tender. Sprinkle with Parmesan cheese, if desired. Makes 6 main-dish servings (8½ cups).

Nutrition facts per serving: 216 calories, 6 g total fat (1 g saturated fat), 0 mg cholesterol, 704 mg sodium, 37 g carbohydrate, 3 g fiber, 9 g protein
Daily Value: 64% vitamin A, 41% vitamin C, 9% calcium, 22% iron

BEAN AND ESCAROLE SOUP

*This hearty white bean soup is a meal in itself when served
with a loaf of crusty bread and a green salad.*

PREPARATION TIME: SOAKING TIME
PLUS 20 MINUTES
COOKING TIME: 17 MINUTES

1⅓ **cups dry great northern
      beans**
  1 **pound smoked ham
      hocks**
  1 **cup celery, sliced
      (2 stalks)**
  1 **cup carrots, sliced
      (2 medium)**
  ⅔ **cup coarsely chopped
      onion**
  2 **cloves garlic, minced**
1½ **teaspoons dried
      oregano, crushed**
  1 **teaspoon dried basil,
      crushed**
2⅔ **cups chicken broth or
      chicken stock (page 36)**
1⅓ **cups water**
  1 **tablespoon cooking oil**
  8 **cups escarole or
      12 ounces fresh
      spinach, shredded
      (1 medium head)**
      **Salt and black pepper to
      taste**

1. Rinse beans. In a large saucepan combine beans and enough water to cover them. Bring to boiling; reduce heat. Simmer for 2 minutes. Remove from heat. Cover and let stand 1 hour. (Or, omit boiling and soak beans overnight.)

2. Drain and rinse the beans. In a 4- or 6-quart pressure cooker combine the beans, ham hocks, celery, carrots, onion, garlic, oregano, basil, chicken broth or chicken stock, water, and oil.

3. Lock lid in place. Place pressure regulator on vent pipe (if you have a first-generation cooker). Over high heat, bring cooker up to pressure. Reduce heat just enough to maintain pressure and pressure regulator rocks gently; cook for 12 minutes.

4. Quick-release the pressure. Carefully remove lid.

5. Remove ham hocks. When cool, remove meat from bones and cut into bite-size pieces. Discard bones.

6. Mash soup mixture slightly with a fork or potato masher. Add escarole or spinach and ham and cook over low heat about 5 minutes or till escarole is tender or spinach is wilted. Season with salt and black pepper to taste. Makes 6 main-dish servings (9 cups).

Nutrition facts per serving: *254 calories, 5 g total fat (1 g saturated fat), 13 mg cholesterol, 776 mg sodium, 35 g carbohydrate, 4 g fiber, 19 g protein*
Daily Value: *107% vitamin A, 51% vitamin C, 15% calcium, 36% iron*

SPICY BEAN SOUP

Spicy chorizo sausage adds flavor to this white bean and vegetable soup.

PREPARATION TIME: SOAKING TIME
FOR BEANS PLUS 15 MINUTES
COOKING TIME: 12 MINUTES

1½ **cups dry navy beans**
8 **ounces chorizo or kielbasa sausage, cut into ¼-inch slices**
1 **cup carrots, peeled and cut into 1-inch pieces (2 medium)**
½ **cup coarsely chopped onion (1 medium)**
½ **cup chopped green sweet pepper**
½ **cup chopped red sweet pepper**
1 **clove garlic, minced**
1 **tablespoon chili powder**
½ **teaspoon dried oregano, crushed**
2 **cups chicken or vegetable broth, chicken stock (page 36), or vegetable stock (page 35)**
1 **cup water**
Chopped green onion (optional)
Chopped tomatoes (optional)

1. Rinse beans. In a large saucepan combine beans and enough water to cover them. Bring to boiling; reduce heat. Simmer for 2 minutes. Remove from heat. Cover and let stand 1 hour. (Or, omit boiling and soak beans overnight.)

2. Drain and rinse the beans. In a 4- or 6-quart pressure cooker place beans, sausage, carrots, onion, sweet peppers, garlic, chili powder, oregano, chicken broth or stock, and water.

3. Lock lid in place. Place pressure regulator on vent pipe (if you have a first-generation cooker). Over high heat, bring cooker up to pressure. Reduce heat just enough to maintain pressure and pressure regulator rocks gently; cook for 12 minutes.

4. Quick-release the pressure. Carefully remove lid.

5. Sprinkle with green onion and tomatoes, if desired. Makes 6 main-dish servings (7 cups).

Nutrition facts per serving: 200 calories, 16 g total fat (6 g saturated fat), 0 mg cholesterol, 291 mg sodium, 36 g carbohydrate, 2 g fiber, 21 g protein
Daily Value: 68% vitamin A, 39% vitamin C, 8% calcium, 22% iron

POTATO CORN SOUP

*This classic soup cooks in a flash and is comfort food at
its best when served up on a chilly night.*

PREPARATION TIME: 15 MINUTES
COOKING TIME: 10 MINUTES

- **4 strips bacon, chopped**
- **1½ cups coarsely chopped onion**
- **1½ cups potatoes, peeled and cut into ½-inch cubes (1 pound)**
- **1 cup coarsely chopped celery (2 stalks)**
- **3 cups fresh or loose-pack frozen corn**
- **2½ cups chicken or vegetable broth, chicken stock (page 36), or vegetable stock (page 35)**
- **2 cups milk or half-and-half**
- **¼ cup snipped fresh parsley**
- **Salt and black pepper to taste**

1. In a 4- or 6-quart pressure cooker cook the bacon till crisp.

2. Add the onion, potatoes, celery, corn, and chicken broth or stock.

3. Lock lid in place. Place pressure regulator on vent pipe (if you have a first-generation cooker). Over high heat, bring cooker up to pressure. Reduce heat just enough to maintain pressure and pressure regulator rocks gently; cook for 3 minutes.

4. Quick-release the pressure. Carefully remove lid. Mash potato mixture slightly with a fork or potato masher.

5. Stir in milk or half-and-half and parsley. Season with salt and black pepper. Heat through. Makes 5 main-dish servings (about 9 cups).

Nutrition facts per serving: 305 calories, 7 g total fat (2 g saturated fat), 12 mg cholesterol, 628 mg sodium, 53 g carbohydrate, 6 g fiber, 13 g protein
Daily Value: 10% vitamin A, 40% vitamin C, 13% calcium, 11% iron

SQUASH, APPLE, AND WILD RICE SOUP

We add cooked wild rice at the end because our test kitchen does not recommend cooking rice under pressure. It can clog the vent pipe during cooking.

PREPARATION TIME: 20 MINUTES
COOKING TIME: 3 MINUTES

3 **cups butternut squash, peeled, seeded, and cut into 1-inch cubes**
1 **cup peeled, coarsely chopped apple (1 large)**
1 **cup thinly sliced leeks**
½ **teaspoon ground ginger**
½ **teaspoon ground nutmeg**
3 **cups chicken broth or chicken stock (page 36)**
1 **cup cooked wild rice Ground nutmeg (optional)**

1. In a 4- or 6-quart pressure cooker combine the squash, apple, leeks, ginger, nutmeg, and chicken broth or stock.

2. Lock lid in place. Place pressure regulator on vent pipe (if you have a first-generation cooker). Over high heat, bring cooker up to pressure. Reduce heat just enough to maintain pressure and pressure regulator rocks gently; cook for 3 minutes.

3. Quick-release the pressure. Carefully remove lid. Mash soup mixture slightly with a fork or potato masher.

4. Add rice to cooker. Heat through. Sprinkle with additional nutmeg, if desired. Makes 4 main-dish servings (6 cups).

Nutrition facts per serving: 264 calories, 2 g total fat (1 g saturated fat), 1 mg cholesterol, 598 mg sodium, 54 g carbohydrate, 6 g fiber, 11 g protein
Daily Value: 67% vitamin A, 33% vitamin C, 7% calcium, 18% iron

Uncooked wild rice keeps indefinitely stored in a cool, dry place or in the refrigerator. If it is cooked with no added ingredients, wild rice keeps, tightly covered, in the refrigerator for several weeks or in the freezer for several months.

Creamy Pumpkin Soup

*A smooth and creamy soup with a hint of ginger, this makes
a perfect first course for a special fall or winter dinner.*

PREPARATION TIME: 20 MINUTES
COOKING TIME: 10 MINUTES

4 **cups fresh pumpkin or
butternut squash,
peeled, seeded, and cut
into 1½-inch pieces
(about 2 pounds)**
¾ **cup sliced leeks or green
onions**
2 **cloves garlic, minced**
½ **teaspoon paprika**
½ **teaspoon ground ginger**
¼ **to ½ teaspoon crushed
red pepper (optional)**
2 **tablespoons soy sauce**
3 **cups chicken broth or
chicken stock (page 36)**
⅓ **cup half-and-half, light
cream, or milk**
2 **tablespoons snipped
fresh cilantro or
parsley**

1. In a 4- or 6-quart pressure cooker combine pumpkin or squash, leeks or green onions, garlic, paprika, ginger, crushed red pepper (if desired), soy sauce, and chicken broth or stock.

2. Lock lid in place. Place pressure regulator on vent pipe (if you have a first-generation cooker). Over high heat, bring cooker up to pressure. Reduce heat just enough to maintain pressure and pressure regulator rocks gently; cook for 5 minutes.

3. Quick-release the pressure. Carefully remove lid.

4. Cool slightly. Place soup mixture, in 2 or 3 batches, in a blender container or food processor bowl. Cover and blend or process till smooth. Return to pressure cooker and stir in half-and-half, light cream, or milk. Heat through. Stir in cilantro or parsley. Makes 6 side-dish servings (5½ cups).

Nutrition facts per serving: 107 calories, 3 g total fat (1 g saturated fat), 6 mg cholesterol, 749 mg sodium, 18 g carbohydrate, 3 g fiber, 5 g protein
Daily Value: *69% vitamin A, 33% vitamin C, 7% calcium, 12% iron*

CHILLED PEPPER SOUP

This delightful appetizer soup can be prepared a day in advance so it can chill to perfection.
It's equally delicious with yellow or red sweet peppers.

PREPARATION TIME: 15 MINUTES
COOKING TIME: 3 MINUTES PLUS
CHILL TIME

- 2½ **cups chopped yellow or red sweet peppers (2 large)**
- ½ **cup chopped onion (1 medium)**
- 1 **clove garlic, minced**
- 1 **teaspoon dried marjoram, crushed**
- 1 **bay leaf**
- 1 **14½-ounce can chicken broth**
- ⅓ **cup dry white wine or chicken broth**
- ¼ **teaspoon black pepper**
- ⅛ **teaspoon salt**
  Sliced green onions

1. In a 4- or 6-quart pressure cooker place the sweet peppers, onion, garlic, marjoram, bay leaf, and 1 can chicken broth.

2. Lock lid in place. Place pressure regulator on vent pipe (if you have a first-generation cooker). Over high heat, bring cooker up to pressure. Reduce heat just enough to maintain pressure and pressure regulator rocks gently; cook for 3 minutes.

3. Quick-release the pressure. Carefully remove lid.

4. Cool mixture slightly. Remove and discard bay leaf. Add ⅓ cup wine or chicken broth, black pepper, and salt. Place soup mixture, in 2 batches, in a blender container or food processor bowl. Cover and blend or process till smooth. Pour into a medium size mixing bowl, cover, and chill at least 4 hours. Sprinkle with green onions. Makes 4 side-dish servings (3½ cups).

Nutrition facts per serving: 55 calories, 1 g total fat (0 g saturated fat), 0 mg cholesterol, 396 mg sodium, 6 g carbohydrate, 1 g fiber, 3 g protein
Daily Value: 2% vitamin A, 59% vitamin C, 1% calcium, 5% iron

Cover and store fresh peppers in your refrigerator for up to 5 days. You can freeze sliced or chopped fresh peppers in freezer bags or containers for up to 6 months.

AFRICAN PEANUT SOUP

Peanuts are called ground nuts in West Africa, where this dish originated. In the country markets there, vendors grind roasted peanuts to a paste that resembles American peanut butter.

PREPARATION TIME: 15 MINUTES
COOKING TIME: 22 MINUTES

2 **tablespoons cooking oil**
1 **pound boneless beef chuck or pork sirloin roast, cut into 1-inch pieces**
1 **cup sliced onion**
½ **cup chopped green sweet pepper**
½ **teaspoon crushed red pepper**
1 **14½-ounce Italian-style plum tomatoes or whole tomatoes, cut up**
½ **cup beef broth or beef stock (page 37)**
¼ **cup peanut butter**
   Salt and black pepper to taste
2 **cups hot cooked rice or noodles**
   Chopped peanuts

1. In a 4- or 6-quart pressure cooker heat 1 tablespoon of the oil over medium heat. Cook meat, half at a time, till brown on all sides. Add more oil, if needed. Remove meat and set aside. Drain off fat.

2. Return all the meat to cooker and add onion, sweet pepper, crushed red pepper, *undrained* tomatoes, and beef broth or stock.

3. Lock lid in place. Place pressure regulator on vent pipe (if you have a first-generation cooker). Over high heat, bring cooker up to pressure. Reduce heat just enough to maintain pressure and pressure regulator rocks gently; cook for 12 minutes.

4. Allow pressure to come down naturally. Carefully remove lid.

5. Add peanut butter to cooker and stir to mix. Season with salt and black pepper to taste. Serve with rice or noodles. Sprinkle with peanuts. Makes 4 main-dish servings (4 cups).

Nutrition facts per serving: 484 calories, 21 g total fat (5 g saturated fat), 82 mg cholesterol, 534 mg sodium, 37 g carbohydrate, 3 g fiber, 37 g protein
Daily Value: 8% vitamin A, 45% vitamin C, 5% calcium, 35% iron

San Francisco Cioppino

This quickly cooked California-style soup features tender chunks of fish, plush shrimp, and crab in an herb-seasoned tomato base. It's ideal for entertaining with a loaf of crusty sourdough bread.

PREPARATION TIME: 15 MINUTES
COOKING TIME: 5 MINUTES

- 1 **pound scrod, cod, or other firm white fish fillets, about 1-inch thick**
- 1 **cup chopped green sweet pepper (1 large)**
- ½ **cup chopped onion**
- 3 **cloves garlic, minced**
- 1½ **teaspoons dried oregano or basil, crushed**
- ¼ **teaspoon black pepper**
- 1 **28-ounce can whole tomatoes, cut up**
- 1 **cup chicken or vegetable broth, chicken stock (page 36), or vegetable stock (page 35)**
- 3 **tablespoons tomato paste**
- ½ **pound medium shrimp, shelled and deveined**
- 1 **6-ounce can crab meat, drained, flaked, and cartilage removed**
- 3 **tablespoons snipped fresh parsley**
  Few dashes bottled hot pepper sauce (optional)

1. Cut fish into 4 pieces. In a 4- or 6-quart pressure cooker combine sweet pepper, onion, garlic, oregano or basil, black pepper, *undrained* tomatoes, chicken broth or stock, and tomato paste. Place fish on top.

2. Lock lid in place. Place pressure regulator on vent pipe (if you have a first-generation cooker). Over high heat, bring cooker up to pressure just till pressure regulator begins to rock slowly.

3. Quick-release the pressure. Carefully remove lid.

4. Add shrimp and crab meat to cooker. Bring to boiling, stirring gently to break up fish fillets. Stir in parsley and hot pepper sauce, if desired. Cook for 1 to 2 minutes or till shrimp turn pink. Makes 6 main-dish servings (8 cups).

Nutrition facts per serving: 164 calories, 2 g total fat (0 g saturated fat), 105 mg cholesterol, 546 mg sodium, 11 g carbohydrate, 2 g fiber, 26 g protein
Daily Value: 14% vitamin A, 67% vitamin C, 8% calcium, 19% iron

SOUTHWEST CHICKEN AND BEAN SOUP

Oil in chili peppers can burn skin and eyes, so avoid direct contact. Wear plastic or rubber gloves, or work under cold running water. If your hands touch the chili peppers, wash your hands well with soap and water.

PREPARATION TIME: SOAKING TIME FOR
BEANS PLUS 15 MINUTES
COOKING TIME: 13 MINUTES

1 **cup dry pinto beans**
1 **cup chopped onion**
2 **jalapeño peppers, seeded
   and chopped**
2 **cloves garlic, minced**
¼ **teaspoon crushed red
   pepper**
2½ **cups chicken broth or
   chicken stock (page 36)**
2 **tablespoons cooking oil**
1 **cup frozen whole kernel
   corn**
2 **cups cubed cooked
   chicken**
1 **16-ounce can whole
   tomatoes, cut up**
¼ **cup snipped fresh
   cilantro or parsley**
   **Shredded cheddar or
   Monterey Jack cheese
   with jalapeño peppers
   (optional)**
   Tortilla chips (optional)
   Lime wedges (optional)

1. Rinse beans. In a large saucepan combine beans and enough water to cover them. Bring to boiling; reduce heat. Simmer for 2 minutes. Remove from heat. Cover and let stand 1 hour. (Or, omit boiling and soak beans overnight.)

2. Drain and rinse the beans. In a 4- or 6-quart pressure cooker combine beans, onion, jalapeño peppers, garlic, crushed red pepper, chicken broth or stock, and oil.

3. Lock lid in place. Place pressure regulator on vent pipe (if you have a first-generation cooker). Over high heat, bring cooker up to pressure. Reduce heat just enough to maintain pressure and pressure regulator rocks gently; cook for 8 minutes.

4. Allow pressure to come down naturally. Carefully remove lid.

5. Add corn to cooker. Bring to boiling; reduce heat. Cover loosely (do not lock lid) and cook about 3 minutes or till corn is tender. Add chicken, *undrained* tomatoes, and cilantro or parsley. Heat through. Sprinkle each serving with cheese, if desired. Serve with tortilla chips and lime wedges, if desired. Make 6 main-dish servings (9 cups).

Nutrition facts per serving: 355 calories, 12 g total fat (2 g saturated fat), 39 mg cholesterol, 489 mg sodium, 38 g carbohydrate, 4 g fiber, 26 g protein
***Daily Value:** 8% vitamin A, 53% vitamin C, 6% calcium, 27% iron*

SAFFRON CHICKEN-VEGETABLE SOUP

In this recipe the pressure cooker produces a rich chicken stock in only 8 minutes. The stock is then strained and combined with the cooked chicken, peas, wild rice, green onions, and tomatoes.

PREPARATION TIME: 25 MINUTES
COOKING TIME: 17 MINUTES

1 to 1¼ **pounds meaty chicken pieces, skinned**
1⅓ **cups celery, cut into 3-inch chunks (2 stalks)**
1 **cup coarsely chopped onion**
1 **cup carrots, cut into 3-inch chunks (1 medium)**
4 **cloves garlic, halved**
2 **sprigs fresh parsley**
4 **whole cloves**
¾ **teaspoon salt**
¾ **teaspoon dried thyme, crushed**
¼ **teaspoon black pepper**
4 **cups water**
⅛ **teaspoon saffron powder or ½ teaspoon ground turmeric**
¼ **teaspoon crushed red pepper (optional)**
1 **cup loose-pack frozen peas**
1 **cup cooked wild or regular rice**
⅓ **cup tomato, seeded and chopped (1 small)**
¼ **cup thinly sliced green onions (2)**

1. In a 4- or 6-quart pressure cooker place chicken pieces, celery, onion, carrot, garlic, parsley, cloves, salt, thyme, black pepper, and water.

2. Lock lid in place. Place pressure regulator on vent pipe (if you have a first-generation cooker). Over high heat, bring cooker up to pressure. Reduce heat just enough to maintain pressure and pressure regulator rocks gently; cook for 8 minutes.

3. Quick-release the pressure. Carefully remove lid. Remove chicken.

4. Pour stock through a large sieve or colander lined with 2 layers of cheesecloth. Discard vegetables and return strained stock to cooker. Add saffron or turmeric and crushed red pepper, if desired. Bring to boiling. Add peas. Reduce heat to low. Cover loosely (do not lock lid) and cook about 5 minutes or till peas are tender.

5. Meanwhile, remove meat from bones and cut into bite-size pieces. Discard bones. Stir chicken, rice, tomato, and green onions into soup and heat through. Makes 4 main-dish servings (6½ cups).

Nutrition facts per serving: 197 calories, 1 g total fat (0 g saturated fat), 0 mg cholesterol, 497 mg sodium, 38 g carbohydrate, 2 g fiber, 10 g protein
Daily Value: 5% vitamin A, 16% vitamin C, 3% calcium, 13% iron

GREEN BEAN AND HAM SOUP

Cubed ham adds an appealing smoky flavor to this very quick soup.

PREPARATION TIME: 20 MINUTES
COOKING TIME: 8 MINUTES

4 **cups fresh green beans,
    cut into 1-inch pieces**
3 **cups potatoes, peeled
    and cut into 1-inch
    cubes**
2 **cups cubed cooked ham**
1 **cup chopped onion
    (1 large)**
4 **cups water**
1 **tablespoon cooking oil**
¼ **cup all-purpose flour**
1 **tablespoon snipped
    fresh dill or 1 teaspoon
    dried dill, crushed**
¼ **teaspoon salt**
¼ **teaspoon black pepper**
1 **cup milk, half-and-half,
    or light cream**

1. In a 4- or 6-quart pressure cooker combine green beans, potatoes, ham, onion, water, and oil.

2. Lock lid in place. Place pressure regulator on vent pipe (if you have a first-generation cooker). Over high heat, bring cooker up to pressure. Reduce heat just enough to maintain pressure and pressure regulator rocks gently; cook for 3 minutes.

3. Quick-release the pressure. Carefully remove lid.

4. Stir together flour, dill, salt, black pepper, and milk, half-and-half, or light cream till smooth. Add to cooker. Cook over medium heat till thickened and bubbly. Cook and stir for 1 minute more. Makes 6 main-dish servings (10 cups).

Nutrition facts per serving: 226 calories, 6 g total fat (2 g saturated fat), 28 mg cholesterol, 682 mg sodium, 30 g carbohydrate, 3 g fiber, 15 g protein
Daily Value: 6% vitamin A, 39% vitamin C, 8% calcium, 13% iron

Beef Goulash Soup

The flavors of classic goulash have been combined in this main-dish soup.
Be sure to use Hungarian paprika—it's more flavorful than regular paprika.

Preparation Time: 16 minutes
Cooking Time: 25 minutes

- 2 **tablespoons cooking oil**
- 1 **pound boneless beef chuck roast, cut into ½-inch pieces**
- 2 **cups potatoes, peeled and cut into ½-inch cubes (2 medium)**
- ¾ **cup chopped onion**
- 2 **cloves garlic, minced**
- 1 **tablespoon snipped fresh thyme or 1 teaspoon dried thyme, crushed**
- 1 **14½-ounce can beef broth**
- 1 **8-ounce can tomato sauce**
- 2 **tablespoons red wine vinegar**
- 2 **teaspoons Worcestershire sauce**
- ¼ **cup all-purpose flour**
- 2 **tablespoons Hungarian sweet paprika**
- ½ **cup water**
- ¾ **cup loose-pack frozen peas**
- ¼ **cup snipped fresh parsley**
- **Salt and pepper to taste**

1. In a 4- or 6-quart pressure cooker heat 1 tablespoon of the oil over medium heat. Cook meat, half at a time, till brown on all sides. Add more oil, if needed. Remove the meat and set aside. Drain off fat.

2. Return all the meat to cooker and add potatoes, onion, garlic, thyme, beef broth, tomato sauce, 1 cup water, vinegar, and Worcestershire sauce.

3. Lock lid in place. Place pressure regulator on vent pipe (if you have a first-generation cooker). Over high heat, bring cooker up to pressure. Reduce heat just enough to maintain pressure and pressure regulator rocks gently; cook for 10 minutes.

4. Allow pressure to come down naturally. Carefully remove lid.

5. Meanwhile, in a small mixing bowl stir together flour, paprika, and ½ cup water. Add peas and parsley to cooker. Slowly add flour mixture to cooker. Cook and stir till thickened and bubbly. Cook and stir for 1 minute more. Season with salt and black pepper to taste. Makes 4 main-dish servings (7½ cups).

Nutrition facts per serving: 444 calories, 16 g total fat (4 g saturated fat), 82 mg cholesterol, 823 mg sodium, 42 g carbohydrate, 4 g fiber, 34 g protein
Daily Value: 28% vitamin A, 46% vitamin C, 5% calcium, 41% iron

CHICKEN AND VEGETABLES WITH COUSCOUS

Couscous is a tiny grainlike pasta from North Africa. A packaged precooked version is found in many supermarkets. In this recipe couscous is added to the cooked chicken stew to steam until tender.

PREPARATION TIME: 10 MINUTES
COOKING TIME: 15 MINUTES

8 **chicken drumsticks and/or thighs (about 2 pounds), skinned**
1½ **cups carrots, peeled and cut into 1-inch pieces (2 large)**
1½ **cups fresh mushrooms, halved**
¾ **cup green sweet pepper, chopped (1 large)**
½ **cup coarsely chopped onion (1 medium)**
2 **cloves garlic, minced**
1 **14½-ounce can stewed tomatoes**
½ **cup chicken broth or chicken stock (page 36)**
1 **cup zucchini, halved lengthwise and thinly sliced (1 small)**
¾ **cup couscous**
   Salt and black pepper to taste
   Snipped fresh parsley

1. In a 4- or 6-quart pressure cooker place chicken, carrots, mushrooms, sweet pepper, onion, garlic, *undrained* tomatoes, and chicken broth or chicken stock.

2. Lock lid in place. Place pressure regulator on vent pipe (if you have a first-generation cooker). Over high heat, bring cooker up to pressure. Reduce heat just enough to maintain pressure and pressure regulator rocks gently; cook for 8 minutes.

3. Quick-release the pressure. Carefully remove lid.

4. Add zucchini and couscous to cooker. Cover loosely (do not lock lid) and let stand about 7 minutes or till couscous is tender. Season with salt and black pepper to taste. Sprinkle with parsley. Makes 4 main-dish servings (5½ cups).

Nutrition facts per serving: *438 calories, 12 g total fat (3 g saturated fat), 98 mg cholesterol, 618 mg sodium, 46 g carbohydrate, 8 g fiber, 35 g protein*
Daily Value: *136% vitamin A, 51% vitamin C, 5% calcium, 20% iron*

Turkey Vegetable Ragout

A ragout is any well-seasoned stew made with meat or poultry.
This one uses inexpensive turkey or chicken thighs.

PREPARATION TIME: 25 MINUTES
COOKING TIME: 34 MINUTES

2¾ **pounds turkey thighs or**
  1½ pounds chicken
  thighs, skinned
2 **cups carrots, cut into**
  2-inch chunks
  (2 medium)
1¼ **cups potato, peeled and**
  cut into 1-inch cubes
  (1 large)
1 **cup sliced celery**
  (2 stalks)
½ **cup chopped onion**
1 **clove garlic, minced**
1 **bay leaf**
1 **teaspoon Italian**
  seasoning, crushed
½ **teaspoon salt**
¼ **teaspoon black pepper**
2 **14½-ounce cans whole**
  Italian-style plum
  tomatoes, cut up
1 **cup water**
1 **tablespoon cooking oil**
1 **10-ounce package frozen**
  succotash
2 **tablespoons snipped**
  fresh parsley

1. Rinse turkey or chicken; pat dry. In a 4- or 6-quart pressure cooker combine carrots, potato, celery, onion, garlic, bay leaf, Italian seasoning, salt, black pepper, 1 can *undrained* tomatoes, water, and oil. Add chicken or turkey.

2. Lock lid in place. Place pressure regulator on vent pipe (if you have a first-generation cooker). Over high heat, bring cooker up to pressure. Reduce heat just enough to maintain pressure and pressure regulator rocks gently; cook for 20 minutes.

3. Quick-release the pressure. Carefully remove lid.

4. Remove chicken or turkey and cool slightly. Add remaining 1 can *undrained* tomatoes, succotash, and parsley to cooker. Bring to boiling. Reduce heat and simmer, uncovered, about 10 minutes. Remove meat from bones and cut into bite-size pieces. Discard bones. Add meat to cooker and heat through. Makes 4 main-dish servings (8 cups).

Nutrition facts per serving: 391 calories, 11 g total fat (3 g saturated fat), 70 mg cholesterol, 749 mg sodium, 46 g carbohydrate, 10 g fiber, 31 g protein
Daily Value: 101% vitamin A, 81% vitamin C, 12% calcium, 35% iron

CURRIED PORK WITH RICE

This curry features fork-tender pork cubes in a sauce seasoned with fresh ginger, garlic, curry powder, and cinnamon. While it cooks, you can prepare the rice and condiments of your choice.

PREPARATION TIME: 20 MINUTES
COOKING TIME: 22 MINUTES

1 **tablespoon cooking oil**
2 **pounds boneless pork sirloin, cut into 1-inch cubes**
4 **cups carrots, peeled and cut into 2-inch chunks**
1 **cup coarsely chopped onion**
2 **cloves garlic, minced**
1 **teaspoon grated gingerroot**
1 **tablespoon curry powder**
½ **teaspoon ground cinnamon**
¼ **teaspoon salt**
⅛ **to ¼ teaspoon ground red pepper**
1⅔ **cups chicken broth or chicken stock (page 36)**
2 **tablespoons flour**
2 **medium apples or pears, coarsely chopped**
   Assorted condiments: raisins, peanuts, chopped tomatoes, toasted coconut, chopped chutney
4½ **cups hot cooked rice**

1. In a 4- or 6-quart pressure cooker heat 1 tablespoon of the oil over medium heat. Cook meat, half at a time, till brown on all sides. Add more oil, if needed. Remove the meat and set aside. Drain off fat.

2. Return all the meat to cooker and add carrots, onion, garlic, gingerroot, curry powder, cinnamon, salt, ground red pepper, and chicken broth or stock.

3. Lock lid in place. Place pressure regulator on vent pipe (if you have a first-generation cooker). Over high heat, bring cooker up to pressure. Reduce heat just enough to maintain pressure and pressure regulator rocks gently; cook for 8 minutes.

4. Allow pressure to come down naturally. Carefully remove lid.

5. Stir together flour and ¼ cup water till well combined. Add to mixture in cooker. Cook and stir till thickened and bubbly. Add apples or pears. Cook about 2 minutes more. Serve with assorted condiments and rice. Makes 6 main-dish servings (6 cups).

Nutrition facts per serving: 523 calories, 23 g total fat (7 g saturated fat), 80 mg cholesterol, 394 mg sodium, 50 g carbohydrate, 3 g fiber, 28 g protein
Daily Value: 114% vitamin A, 9% vitamin C, 4% calcium, 22% iron

Beef Bourguignon

*This version of the classic French country beef stew is ideal
when you need a quick meal for company.*

Preparation Time: 20 minutes
Cooking Time: 17 minutes

1½ pounds lean boneless
      beef chuck roast, cut
      into 1-inch pieces
  4 medium carrots, peeled
      and cut into thirds
      crosswise
2⅔ cups fresh mushrooms,
      halved (8 ounces)
  ¾ cup onion, cut into
      wedges (1 medium)
  2 cloves garlic, minced
  1 bay leaf
  ¾ teaspoon salt
  ½ teaspoon dried thyme,
      crushed
  ¼ teaspoon black pepper
  ⅔ cup beef broth, beef
      stock (page 37), or
      water
  ⅔ cup dry red wine
  2 tablespoons tomato
      paste
  2 tablespoons flour
  ¼ cup snipped fresh
      parsley
  6 cups hot cooked
      spaghetti, linguine, or
      other pasta (12-ounces
      uncooked)

1. In a 4- or 6-quart pressure cooker combine beef, carrots, mushrooms, onion, garlic, bay leaf, salt, thyme, black pepper, ⅔ cup beef broth, beef stock, or water, wine, and tomato paste.

2. Lock lid in place. Place pressure regulator on vent pipe (if you have a first-generation cooker). Over high heat, bring cooker up to pressure. Reduce heat just enough to maintain pressure and pressure regulator rocks gently; cook for 12 minutes.

3. Allow pressure to come down naturally. Carefully remove lid.

4. Remove the bay leaf and discard. In a small bowl stir together flour and ¼ cup water till well combined. Add to mixture in cooker. Cook and stir till thickened and bubbly. Cook and stir for 1 minute more. Stir in parsley. Serve over noodles. Makes 6 main-dish servings (about 6 cups).

Nutrition facts per serving: 460 calories, 11 g total fat (4 g saturated fat), 131 mg cholesterol, 472 mg sodium, 49 g carbohydrate, 3 g fiber, 36 g protein
Daily Value: 117% vitamin A, 15% vitamin C, 5% calcium, 47% iron

BEEF STEW WITH VEGETABLES

Stews can take hours in a slow oven—or minutes in a pressure cooker.
Vegetable juice cocktail is the flavorful liquid used here.

PREPARATION TIME: 20 MINUTES
COOKING TIME: 22 MINUTES

- **2 tablespoons all-purpose flour**
- **1 pound beef chuck or pork shoulder roast, cut into 1-inch pieces**
- **2 tablespoons cooking oil**
- **2 cups celery, cut into 2-inch pieces (2 stalks)**
- **2 cups carrots, peeled and cut into 1-inch pieces (4 medium)**
- **1½ cups potatoes, peeled and cut into 1-inch pieces (3 medium)**
- **1 cup cubed, peeled turnips (1-inch)**
- **½ cup coarsely chopped onion (1 medium)**
- **2 cloves garlic, minced**
- **1 teaspoon dried basil, crushed**
- **½ teaspoon dried thyme, crushed**
- **1 bay leaf**
- **1½ cups vegetable juice cocktail**
- **Salt and black pepper to taste**
- **Snipped fresh chives or parsley**

1. Place flour in a plastic bag. Add meat, a few pieces at a time, shaking to coat. In a 4- or 6-quart pressure cooker heat 1 tablespoon of the oil over medium heat. Cook meat, half at a time, till brown on all sides. Add more oil, if needed. Remove meat and set aside. Drain off fat.

2. Return all the meat to cooker and add celery, carrots, potatoes, turnips, onion, garlic, basil, thyme, bay leaf, and vegetable juice cocktail.

3. Lock lid in place. Place pressure regulator on vent pipe (if you have a first-generation cooker). Over high heat, bring cooker up to pressure. Reduce heat just enough to maintain pressure and pressure regulator rocks gently; cook for 12 minutes.

4. Allow pressure to come down naturally. Carefully remove lid.

5. Season with salt and black pepper to taste. Sprinkle with chives or parsley. Makes 4 main-dish servings (7 cups).

Nutrition facts per serving: *405 calories, 12 g total fat (4 g saturated fat), 82 mg cholesterol, 564 mg sodium, 43 g carbohydrate, 6 g fiber, 32 g protein*
Daily Value: *182% vitamin A, 73% vitamin C, 7% calcium, 33% iron*

LAMB AND LENTIL STEW

For a robust winter supper, serve this nicely seasoned stew featuring tender chunks of lamb, lentils, bits of carrots, diced tomatoes, and fresh spinach with crusty bread or rolls.

PREPARATION TIME: 20 MINUTES
COOKING TIME: 22 MINUTES

2   tablespoons cooking oil
1¼   pounds boneless lamb
       shoulder, cut into
       1-inch cubes
1⅓   cups dry lentils, rinsed
1   cup coarsely chopped
       onion
1   cup carrots, peeled and
       chopped (2 medium)
2   cloves garlic, minced
1   teaspoon dried basil,
       crushed
½   teaspoon salt
¼   teaspoon black pepper
1   14½-ounce can diced
       peeled tomatoes
1½   cups water
3   cups torn spinach

1. In a 4- or 6-quart pressure cooker heat 1 tablespoon of the oil over medium heat. Cook meat, half at a time, till brown on all sides. Add more oil, if needed. Remove the meat and set aside. Drain off fat.

2. Return all the meat to cooker and add lentils, onion, carrots, garlic, basil, salt, black pepper, *undrained* tomatoes, and water.

3. Lock lid in place. Place pressure regulator on vent pipe (if you have a first-generation cooker). Over high heat, bring cooker up to pressure. Reduce heat just enough to maintain pressure and pressure regulator rocks gently; cook for 12 minutes.

4. Allow pressure to come down naturally. Carefully remove lid.

5. Stir in the spinach till it begins to wilt. Makes 6 main-dish servings (7 cups).

Nutrition facts per serving: 361 calories, 14 g total fat (5 g saturated fat), 53 mg cholesterol, 385 mg sodium, 34 g carbohydrate, 4 g fiber, 26 g protein
Daily Value: 136% vitamin A, 38% vitamin C, 8% calcium, 42% iron

Black Bean Chili with Salsa

If you like a thicker soup, slightly mash some of the beans before serving. The tomato salsa adds both flavor and color to this chili. Serve with warm tortillas or corn bread.

Preparation Time: soaking time for beans plus 20 minutes
Cooking Time: 12 minutes

- **2 cups dry black beans**
- **1 tablespoon cooking oil**
- **1 cup coarsely chopped onion**
- **¾ cup diced red sweet pepper (1 medium)**
- **¾ cup diced green sweet pepper (1 medium)**
- **4 cloves garlic, minced**
- **2 to 4 jalapeño peppers, seeded and thinly sliced**
- **2 tablespoons chili powder**
- **1 teaspoon ground cumin**
- **½ teaspoon salt**
- **¼ teaspoon black pepper**
- **3 cups water**
- **Tomato Salsa**
- **Dairy sour cream (optional)**

1. Rinse beans. In a large saucepan combine beans and enough water to cover them. Bring to boiling; reduce heat. Simmer for 2 minutes. Remove from heat. Cover and let stand 1 hour. (Or, omit boiling and soak beans overnight.)

2. Drain and rinse the beans. In a 4- or 6-quart pressure cooker combine the beans, onion, sweet peppers, garlic, jalapeño peppers, chili powder, cumin, salt, black pepper, and water.

3. Lock lid in place. Place pressure regulator on vent pipe (if you have a first-generation cooker). Over high heat, bring cooker up to pressure. Reduce heat just enough to maintain pressure and pressure regulator rocks gently; cook for 12 minutes.

4. Quick-release the pressure. Carefully remove lid. Serve with Tomato Salsa and sour cream, if desired. Makes 4 main-dish servings (6⅔ cups).

TOMATO SALSA: In a medium mixing bowl stir together 4 medium *plum tomatoes* (chopped), ½ cup chopped *green sweet pepper*, ½ ripe *avocado* (seeded, peeled, and finely chopped), 2 *green onions* (chopped), 2 tablespoons *lime juice*, and 1 tablespoon *snipped fresh cilantro*. Makes about 1½ cups.

Nutrition facts per serving: 419 calories, 10 g total fat (1 g saturated fat), 0 mg cholesterol, 325 mg sodium, 68 g carbohydrate, 9 g fiber, 22 g protein
Daily Value: 37% vitamin A, 172% vitamin C, 9% calcium, 45% iron

Cincinnati-Style Turkey Chili

*This version of Cincinnati chili starts with ground turkey
or chicken and is flavored with six different spices.*

Preparation Time: 20 minutes
Cooking Time: 15 minutes

- 2 **tablespoons cooking oil**
- 1 **pound ground raw turkey or chicken**
- 1 **cup coarsely chopped onion (1 large)**
- 1 **clove garlic, minced**
- 1 **tablespoon chili powder**
- ½ **teaspoon paprika**
- ½ **teaspoon ground cumin**
- ¼ **teaspoon salt**
- ¼ **teaspoon ground cinnamon**
- ⅛ **teaspoon ground cloves**
- ⅛ **teaspoon ground red pepper**
- 1 **14½-ounce can stewed tomatoes**
- 1 **8-ounce can tomato sauce**
- ½ **6-ounce can tomato paste**
- ¼ **cup water**
- 1 **15½-ounce can red kidney beans, drained**
- 3 **cups hot cooked spaghetti**
- ½ **cup chopped onion**
- ½ **cup dairy sour cream**
- ⅓ **cup shredded cheddar cheese**

1. In a 4- or 6-quart pressure cooker heat 1 tablespoon of the oil over medium heat. Cook meat, half at a time, till brown on all sides. Add more oil, if needed. Remove the meat and set aside. Drain off fat.

2. Add 1 cup onion, garlic, chili powder, paprika, cumin, salt, cinnamon, cloves, ground red pepper, *undrained* stewed tomatoes, tomato sauce, tomato paste, and water.

3. Lock lid in place. Place pressure regulator on vent pipe (if you have a first-generation cooker). Over high heat, bring cooker up to pressure. Reduce heat just enough to maintain pressure and pressure regulator rocks gently; cook for 5 minutes.

4. Allow pressure to come down naturally or quick-release the pressure. Carefully remove lid.

5. Add beans and cook over low heat till beans are heated through. Serve over spaghetti. Top with onion, sour cream, and cheese. Makes 6 main-dish servings (6 cups).

Nutrition facts per serving: 395 calories, 14 g total fat (5 g saturated fat), 42 mg cholesterol, 759 mg sodium, 48 g carbohydrate, 7 g fiber, 23 g protein
Daily Value: 21% vitamin A, 26% vitamin C, 11% calcium, 28% iron

Mixed Bean and Sausage Chili

Prepare this flavorful chili when you expect six hungry people—it yields 11 cups.
If they like a hot spicy bean chili, be sure to add the crushed red pepper.

Preparation Time: soaking time for
beans plus 20 minutes
Cooking Time: 23 minutes

- 2 **cups mixed dry beans (garbanzo, navy, and pinto)**
- 1 **pound sweet or hot Italian sausage, casings removed, if desired, and cut into 1-inch chunks**
- 1½ **cups chopped onions**
- 2 **cloves garlic, minced**
- 2 **tablespoons chili powder**
- 2 **teaspoons dried oregano leaves, crushed**
- 1 **teaspoon ground cumin**
- 1 **teaspoon crushed red pepper (optional)**
- 2 **14½-ounce cans stewed tomatoes**
- 1 **12-ounce bottle beer or 1½ cups water**
- ½ **cup water**
- 2 **tablespoons tomato paste**
- ¼ **cup snipped fresh cilantro (optional)**
  Shredded cheddar cheese (optional)

1. Rinse beans. In a large saucepan combine beans and enough water to cover them. Bring to boiling; reduce heat. Simmer for 2 minutes. Remove from heat. Cover and let stand 1 hour. (Or, omit boiling and soak beans overnight.)

2. In a 4- or 6-quart pressure cooker, cook meat, half at a time, till brown. Remove the meat and set aside. Drain off fat.

3. Drain and rinse the beans. Add beans, onion, garlic, chili powder, oregano, cumin, crushed red pepper (if desired) *undrained* tomatoes, beer or 1½ cups water, ½ cup water, and tomato paste.

4. Lock lid in place. Place pressure regulator on vent pipe (if you have a first-generation cooker). Over high heat, bring cooker up to pressure. Reduce heat just enough to maintain pressure and pressure regulator rocks gently; cook for 18 minutes.

5. Quick-release the pressure. Carefully remove lid.

6. If mixture is too thin, cook, uncovered, over low heat till chili is desired consistency. Stir in cilantro, if desired. Sprinkle with cheese, if desired. Makes 6 main-dish servings (11 cups).

Nutrition facts per serving: *465 calories, 16 g total fat (5 g saturated fat), 43 mg cholesterol, 976 mg sodium, 54 g carbohydrate, 4 g fiber, 25 g protein*
Daily Value: *15% vitamin A, 30% vitamin C, 11% calcium, 37% iron*

DILLED SHRIMP CHOWDER

If you would like a dilled clam chowder, omit the shrimp and add 2 cans of undrained minced clams.
A nice way to end the meal might include fresh fruit for dessert.

PREPARATION TIME: 21 MINUTES
COOKING TIME: 8 MINUTES

- 4 **cups cubed peeled potatoes**
- 1 **cup chopped onion (1 large)**
- 1 **cup chopped celery (2 stalks)**
- 1 **bay leaf**
- 1½ **cups chicken broth or chicken stock (page 36)**
- 2 **cups half-and-half, light cream, or milk**
- 2 **tablespoons all-purpose flour**
- 1 **pound medium shrimp, peeled and deveined**
- 1 **6½-ounce can minced clams**
- 2 **tablespoons snipped fresh dill or 1 teaspoon dried dillweed**
- **Dairy sour cream (optional)**

1. In a 4- or 6-quart pressure cooker combine potatoes, onion, celery, bay leaf, and chicken broth or stock.

2. Lock lid in place. Place pressure regulator on vent pipe (if you have a first-generation cooker). Over high heat, bring cooker up to pressure. Reduce heat just enough to maintain pressure and pressure regulator rocks gently; cook for 2 minutes.

3. Quick-release the pressure. Carefully remove lid. Remove bay leaf. Slightly mash potatoes with a fork or potato masher.

4. In a medium mixing bowl stir together the half-and-half, light cream, or milk and the flour. Add to cooker. Stir in shrimp and *undrained* clams. Cook and stir till slightly thickened and bubbly. Cook and stir for 1 minute more or till shrimp are done. Stir in dill. Dollop with sour cream, if desired. Makes 6 main-dish servings (9 cups).

Nutrition facts per serving: 293 calories, 11 g total fat (6 g saturated fat), 151 mg cholesterol, 393 mg sodium, 31 g carbohydrate, 2 g fiber, 20 g protein
Daily Value: 15% vitamin A, 21% vitamin C, 12% calcium, 24% iron

VEGETABLE STOCK

Imagine a full-flavored vegetable broth that cooks under pressure in just 10 minutes.
It's the perfect choice when you need lots of flavor but want zero fat.

PREPARATION TIME: 20 MINUTES
COOKING TIME: 10 MINUTES

2 **cups chopped onions
(4 medium)**
2 **cups chopped carrots
(4 medium)**
1 **cup sliced celery
(2 medium stalks)**
2 **bay leaves**
1½ **teaspoons salt**
1 **teaspoon dried oregano,
crushed**
8 **whole black
peppercorns**
8 **cups water**

1. In a 6-quart pressure cooker combine onions, carrots, celery, bay leaf, salt, oregano, black peppercorns, and water.

2. Lock lid in place. Place pressure regulator on vent pipe (if you have a first-generation cooker). Over high heat, bring cooker up to pressure. Reduce heat just enough to maintain pressure and pressure regulator rocks gently; cook for 10 minutes.

3. Allow pressure to come down naturally. Carefully remove lid.

4. Pour stock through a large sieve or colander lined with 2 layers of cheesecloth. Discard vegetables and seasonings. Store stock in covered containers in the refrigerator up to 3 days or in freezer up to 3 months. Makes 7 cups.

NOTE: If using a 4-quart pressure cooker, halve the ingredients.

Nutrition facts per serving: 27 calories, 0 g total fat (0 g saturated fat), 0 mg cholesterol,
496 mg sodium, 6 g carbohydrate, 1 g fiber, 1 g protein
Daily Value: 67% vitamin A, 4% vitamin C, 2% calcium, 2% iron

Chicken Stock

For richer color, use an unpeeled yellow onion.

Preparation Time: 20 minutes
Cooking Time: 30 minutes

2½ **pounds chicken backs, necks, and wings**
2 **cups celery with leaves, cut into 1-inch pieces (3 stalks)**
1 **cup carrots, cut into 1-inch pieces (2 medium)**
1 **cup sliced onion**
2 **sprigs fresh parsley**
½ **teaspoon salt**
½ **teaspoon dried thyme, sage, or basil, crushed**
5 **whole black peppercorns**
2 **bay leaves**
8 **cups water**

If time permits, chill stock first. Then you can easily skim off fat layer. Use this stock as a base for your favorite soup or stew or any recipe in this cookbook that calls for chicken broth.

1. In a 6-quart pressure cooker combine chicken, celery, carrots, onion, parsley, salt, thyme, black peppercorns, bay leaves, and water.

2. Lock lid in place. Place pressure regulator on vent pipe (if you have a first-generation cooker). Over high heat, bring cooker up to pressure. Reduce heat just enough to maintain pressure and pressure regulator rocks gently; cook for 30 minutes.

3. Allow pressure to come down naturally. Carefully remove lid.

4. Pour stock through a large sieve or colander lined with 2 layers of cheesecloth. Discard bones, vegetables, and seasonings. (If desired, reserve and freeze meat for another use.) Store stock in covered containers in the refrigerator up to 3 days or in freezer up to 3 months. Makes about 7 cups.

NOTE: If using a 4-quart pressure cooker, halve the ingredients.

Nutrition facts per cup: 23 calories, 1 g total fat (0 g saturated fat), 0 mg cholesterol, 217 mg sodium, 2 g carbohydrate, 0 g fiber, 2 g protein
***Daily Value:** 0% vitamin A, 0% vitamin C, 1% calcium, 3% iron*

BEEF STOCK

Use meaty beef bones to make this stock, such as beef shank crosscuts, short ribs, knuckle,
or marrow bones. Trim off as much fat as possible from the meat for a lower-fat broth.

PREPARATION TIME: 10 MINUTES
COOKING TIME: 55 MINUTES

- **2 teaspoons cooking oil**
- **3 pounds meaty beef soup bones**
- **1½ cups carrots, cut into 1-inch pieces (3 medium)**
- **2 cups celery, cut into 1-inch pieces (3 stalks)**
- **2 bay leaves**
- **1⅓ cups sliced onion**
- **¾ teaspoon dried thyme, crushed**
- **1½ teaspoons salt**
- **7 whole black peppercorns**
- **8 cups water**

To clarify stock, combine stock, ¼ cup cold water, and an egg white after reducing the pressure. Bring to boiling. Then remove from heat and let stand 5 minutes before straining through a colander lined with cheesecloth as directed in step 5.

1. In a 6-quart pressure cooker heat 1 tablespoon of the oil over medium heat. Cook bones, half at a time, till brown on all sides. Add more oil, if needed. Remove the meat from bones and set aside. Drain off fat.

2. Add carrots, celery, bay leaves, onion, thyme, salt, black peppercorns, and water.

3. Lock lid in place. Place pressure regulator on vent pipe (if you have a first-generation cooker). Over high heat, bring cooker up to pressure. Reduce heat just enough to maintain pressure and pressure regulator rocks gently; cook for 45 minutes.

4. Allow pressure to come down naturally. Carefully remove lid.

5. Pour stock through a large sieve or colander lined with 2 layers of cheesecloth. Discard bones, vegetables, and seasonings. (If desired, reserve and freeze meat for another use.) Store stock in covered containers in the refrigerator up to 3 days or in freezer up to 3 months. Makes about 6¾ cups.

Note: If using a 4-quart pressure cooker, halve the ingredients.

Nutrition facts per serving: 43 calories, 1 g total fat (0 g saturated fat), 0 mg cholesterol, 515 mg sodium, 7 g carbohydrate, 2 g fiber, 1 g protein
Daily Value: *73% vitamin A, 6% vitamin C, 3% calcium, 3% iron*

RASPBERRY-GLAZED CHICKEN

Raspberry preserves and fresh ginger flavor this elegant but easy chicken dish.
For a special touch, serve with rice pilaf.

PREPARATION TIME: 20 MINUTES
COOKING TIME: 8 MINUTES

1½ to 2 pounds meaty
    chicken pieces (breasts,
    thighs, and drumsticks)
¾ cup seedless raspberry
    preserves
 2 teaspoons grated
    gingerroot
 2 tablespoons red wine
    vinegar
¼ cup chicken broth or
    chicken stock (page 36)
⅓ cup seedless raspberry
    preserves
 2 tablespoons sliced green
    onions

1. Skin chicken; rinse and pat dry. Set aside. For glaze, in a small mixing bowl stir together the ¾ cup raspberry preserves, gingerroot, and vinegar. Brush some of the glaze on the chicken.

2. In a 4- or 6-quart pressure cooker place the chicken, chicken broth or stock, and any remaining glaze.

3. Lock lid in place. Place pressure regulator on vent pipe (if you have a first-generation cooker). Over high heat, bring cooker up to pressure. Reduce heat just enough to maintain pressure and pressure regulator rocks gently; cook for 8 minutes.

4. Quick-release the pressure. Carefully remove lid. Transfer chicken to a serving platter; keep warm.

5. In a small saucepan melt the remaining ⅓ cup raspberry preserves over low heat. Drizzle over chicken and sprinkle with green onions. Makes 4 main-dish servings.

Nutrition facts per serving: *383 calories, 6 g total fat (2 g saturated fat), 69 mg cholesterol, 121 mg sodium, 61 g carbohydrate, 1 g fiber, 23 g protein*
Daily Value: *1% vitamin A, 3% vitamin C, 2% calcium, 12% iron*

GARLIC CHICKEN

Garlic lovers may want to increase the garlic in this recipe from 10 to 15 cloves (pictured on cover).

PREPARATION TIME: 21 MINUTES
COOKING TIME: 20 MINUTES

1½ **pounds skinless,**
    boneless chicken
    breasts and/or thighs
10 **medium cloves garlic**
 ½ **teaspoon lemon-pepper**
    seasoning
 ½ **cup chicken broth or**
    chicken stock (page 36)
 ¼ **cup dry white wine,**
    chicken broth, or
    chicken stock (page 36)
 4 **cups broccoli flowerets**
 2 **tablespoons snipped**
    fresh basil or
    1 teaspoon dried basil,
    crushed
 2 **teaspoons cornstarch**
 1 **tablespoon water**
 ½ **cup chopped walnuts,**
    pecans, or almonds,
    toasted
    Red sweet pepper strips
    (optional)

1. Rinse chicken and pat dry. In a 4- or 6-quart pressure cooker combine chicken, garlic, lemon-pepper seasoning, chicken broth or stock, and wine.

2. Lock lid in place. Place pressure regulator on vent pipe (if you have a first-generation cooker). Over high heat, bring cooker up to pressure. Reduce heat just enough to maintain pressure and pressure regulator rocks gently; cook for 8 minutes.

3. Quick-release the pressure. Carefully remove lid. Transfer chicken to a serving platter; keep warm.

4. Add the broccoli and basil to the cooker. Bring to boiling; reduce heat. Loosely cover (do not lock lid) and simmer for 5 to 7 minutes or till broccoli is crisp-tender. With slotted spoon remove broccoli to serving platter.

5. In a small mixing bowl stir together cornstarch and water; add to cooker. Cook and stir till thickened and bubbly. Spoon over chicken and broccoli. Sprinkle with nuts. If desired, garnish with sweet pepper strips. Makes 6 main-dish servings.

Nutrition facts per serving: 232 calories, 10 g total fat (2 g saturated fat), 60 mg cholesterol, 235 mg sodium, 9 g carbohydrate, 4 g fiber, 26 g protein
Daily Value: 13% vitamin A, 115% vitamin C, 6% calcium, 12% iron

STUFFED CHICKEN BREASTS

Each tender breast is stuffed with a mix of mushrooms, bread crumbs, sage, marjoram, and just a hint of garlic.
You can prepare the chicken rolls in advance and chill until time to pressure-cook them.

PREPARATION TIME: 25 MINUTES
COOKING TIME: 10 MINUTES

- 4 **skinless, boneless chicken breast halves (about 1 pound)**
- 1 **2½-ounce jar sliced mushrooms, drained**
- ½ **cup fine dry bread crumbs**
- ½ **teaspoon dried sage, crushed**
- ¼ **teaspoon dried marjoram, crushed**
  Dash garlic salt
  Dash black pepper
- 2 **tablespoons chicken broth or chicken stock (page 36)**
- ½ **cup chicken broth or chicken stock (page 36)**
- 1 **tablespoon cornstarch**
- 1 **tablespoon dry white wine**

1. Rinse chicken and pat dry. Place each chicken breast half between 2 sheets of plastic wrap. Working from center to the edges, pound lightly with the flat side of a meat mallet to ⅛-inch thickness. Set aside.

2. In a small mixing bowl stir together mushrooms, bread crumbs, sage, marjoram, garlic salt, black pepper, and 2 tablespoons chicken broth or stock. Spoon one-fourth of the mixture onto the short end of each chicken breast. Fold in long sides of chicken and roll up, jelly-roll style, starting from the short edge. Secure with wooden toothpicks. Place in a 4- or 6-quart pressure cooker and add ½ cup chicken broth or stock.

3. Lock lid in place. Place pressure regulator on vent pipe (if you have a first-generation cooker). Over high heat, bring cooker up to pressure. Reduce heat just enough to maintain pressure and pressure regulator rocks gently; cook for 5 minutes.

4. Quick-release the pressure. Carefully remove lid. Remove chicken to a serving platter; keep warm.

5. For sauce, strain liquid in cooker through a sieve; return liquid to cooker. In a small bowl stir together cornstarch and wine. Add to liquid in cooker. Cook and stir till thickened and bubbly. Cook and stir for 2 minutes more. Serve sauce over chicken. Makes 4 main-dish servings.

Nutrition facts per serving: *191 calories, 4 g total fat (1 g saturated fat), 60 mg cholesterol, 375 mg sodium, 12 g carbohydrate, 1 g fiber, 24 g protein*
Daily Value: *0% vitamin A, 0% vitamin C, 2% calcium, 9% iron*

CHICKEN AND RAVIOLI WITH ASPARAGUS

This one-dish meal starts with boneless chicken and fresh cheese ravioli.
It's ready in less than 30 minutes from start to finish.

PREPARATION TIME: 20 MINUTES
COOKING TIME: 8 MINUTES

8 ounces skinless, boneless chicken breast halves
1 10-ounce package frozen cut asparagus
½ cup finely chopped onion
1 teaspoon dried oregano, crushed
½ teaspoon dried tarragon, crushed
2 cups chicken broth or chicken stock (page 36)
3 tablespoons all-purpose flour
Dash black pepper
1 5-ounce can evaporated milk
1 tablespoon margarine or butter, melted
1 9-ounce package refrigerated cheese-filled ravioli or tortellini
¼ cup grated Parmesan or Romano cheese

1. Rinse chicken and pat dry. Cut into bite-size strips.

2. In a 4- or 6-quart pressure cooker combine the chicken, asparagus, onion, oregano, tarragon, and 1 cup of the chicken broth or stock.

3. Lock lid in place. Place pressure regulator on vent pipe (if you have a first-generation cooker). Over high heat, bring cooker up to pressure. Reduce heat just enough to maintain pressure and pressure regulator rocks gently; cook for 30 minutes.

4. Quick-release the pressure. Carefully remove lid. With slotted spoon remove chicken and asparagus; set aside. Add remaining 1 cup chicken broth or stock to cooker. Bring to boiling. Stir in ravioli or tortellini and cook 5 to 6 minutes or till tender.

5. In a small mixing bowl stir together flour, black pepper, evaporated milk, and margarine; stir into cooker. Cook and stir over medium heat till thickened and bubbly. Cook and stir for 1 minute more. Return chicken and asparagus to cooker. Stir in cheese. Heat through. If desired, sprinkle each serving with additional cheese. Makes 6 main-dish servings.

Nutrition facts per serving: 229 calories, 10 g total fat (4 g saturated fat), 53 mg cholesterol, 516 mg sodium, 18 g carbohydrate, 1 g fiber, 19 g protein
Daily Value: 9% vitamin A, 21% vitamin C, 17% calcium, 11% iron

CREAMY CHICKEN WITH CORNMEAL DUMPLINGS

We've redesigned old-fashioned chicken and dumplings for the '90s.
Light cornmeal dumplings top this hearty chicken stew that cooks in just 15 minutes.

PREPARATION TIME: 15 MINUTES
COOKING TIME: 15 MINUTES

- **12 ounces skinless, boneless chicken breast halves**
- **2 cups desired fresh vegetables, such as chopped carrots, chopped turnip, chopped rutabaga, chopped onion, and/or green beans cut into 1-inch pieces**
- **1 9-ounce package frozen whole kernel corn**
- **1 clove garlic, minced**
- **½ teaspoon salt**
- **½ teaspoon dried basil, crushed**
- **¼ teaspoon dried mustard**
- **⅛ teaspoon black pepper**
- **1 cup vegetable broth, vegetable stock (page 35), or water**
  Cornmeal Dumplings
- **¼ cup all-purpose flour**
- **¾ cup milk**

1. Rinse chicken and pat dry. Cut into ¾-inch pieces. In a 4- or 6-quart pressure cooker combine chicken, desired vegetables, corn, garlic, salt, basil, mustard, black pepper, and vegetable broth or stock or water.

2. Lock lid in place. Place pressure regulator on vent pipe (if you have a first-generation cooker). Over high heat, bring cooker up to pressure. Reduce heat just enough to maintain pressure and pressure regulator rocks gently; cook for 3 minutes. While mixture cooks, prepare the batter for Cornmeal Dumplings and set aside.

3. Quick-release the pressure. Carefully remove lid.

4. In a small mixing bowl stir together the flour and milk; add to the pressure cooker. Cook and stir over medium heat till thickened and bubbly. Drop dumpling batter from a tablespoon to make 4 mounds atop bubbling chicken mixture. Cover loosely (do not lock lid) and simmer for 10 to 12 minutes or till a wooden toothpick inserted near center of dumpling comes out clean. Makes 4 main-dish servings.

CORNMEAL DUMPLINGS: In a small bowl stir together ⅓ cup *all-purpose flour*, ⅓ cup *yellow cornmeal*, 1 teaspoon *baking powder*, ⅛ teaspoon *salt*, and dash *black pepper*. Combine ¼ cup *milk* and 2 tablespoons *cooking oil*; add to flour mixture, stirring just till combined.

Nutrition facts per serving: *387 calories, 12 g total fat (3 g saturated fat), 49 mg cholesterol, 793 mg sodium, 50 g carbohydrate, 4 g fiber, 24 g protein*
Daily Value: *241% vitamin A, 10% vitamin C, 17% calcium, 20% iron*

WARM CHICKEN SALAD

While the chicken and apricots cook, you can shred the cheese and tear the lettuce for this easy salad.

PREPARATION TIME: 10 MINUTES
COOKING TIME: 4 MINUTES

4 **skinless, boneless chicken breast halves**
¾ **cup snipped dried apricots**
3 **inches stick cinnamon**
½ **teaspoon finely shredded orange peel**
¼ **teaspoon ground cloves**
¾ **cup orange juice**
¼ **cup water**
½ **cup pecans, toasted**
½ **cup finely shredded mozzarella cheese (2 ounces)**
8 **cups torn leaf lettuce**

To toast pecans, spread the pecans into a thin layer in a shallow baking pan. Bake in a 350° oven for 5 to 10 minutes or till light golden brown, stirring once or twice.

1. Rinse chicken and pat dry. In a 4- or 6-quart pressure cooker combine chicken, apricots, cinnamon, orange peel, cloves, orange juice, and water.

2. Lock lid in place. Place pressure regulator on vent pipe (if you have a first-generation cooker). Over high heat, bring cooker up to pressure. Reduce heat just enough to maintain pressure and pressure regulator rocks gently; cook for 4 minutes.

3. Quick-release the pressure. Carefully remove lid. With a slotted spoon remove chicken and apricots.

4. Cut chicken into bite-size strips. Line 4 salad plates with lettuce; arrange chicken, apricots, pecans, and cheese over lettuce. Remove cinnamon stick from the juices and discard. Drizzle cooking juices over each salad. Makes 4 main-dish servings.

Nutrition facts per serving: 286 calories, 14 g total fat (3 g saturated fat), 38 mg cholesterol, 106 mg sodium, 27 g carbohydrate, 5 g fiber, 18 g protein
Daily Value: 42% vitamin A, 73% vitamin C, 16% calcium, 23% iron

PORK POT ROAST WITH APPLES

Cooked apple wedges make a delicious accompaniment to this tender pork roast.
Serve tangy sauerkraut on the side.

PREPARATION TIME: 10 MINUTES
COOKING TIME: 60 MINUTES

- 1 2½- to 3-pound pork shoulder roast
- 1 teaspoon caraway seed, crushed
- ½ teaspoon salt
- ½ teaspoon black pepper
- 2 tablespoons cooking oil
- 1 medium onion, cut into wedges
- 1 cup water
- ¾ cup apple cider or apple juice
- 3 medium cooking apples, cut into wedges

1. Trim any visible fat from the meat. Set aside. In a small mixing bowl combine caraway seed, salt, and black pepper. Rub over meat.

2. In a 4- or 6-quart pressure cooker heat 1 tablespoon of the oil over medium heat. Cook meat till brown on all sides. Add more oil, if needed. Remove the meat and set aside. Drain off fat.

3. Place the rack in the pressure cooker. Return the meat to the pressure cooker and add the onion, water, and apple cider or apple juice.

4. Lock lid in place. Place pressure regulator on vent pipe (if you have a first-generation cooker). Over high heat, bring cooker up to pressure. Reduce heat just enough to maintain pressure and pressure regulator rocks gently; cook for 45 minutes.

5. Allow pressure to come down naturally. Carefully remove lid. Transfer meat and onion to a serving platter; keep warm.

6. Add apples to pressure cooker. Bring to boiling. Cover loosely (do not lock lid) and cook over medium heat about 5 minutes or till apples are crisp-tender. With a slotted spoon, remove apples to serving platter. Makes 8 main-dish servings.

Nutrition facts per serving: *245 calories, 14 g total fat (4 g saturated fat), 74 mg cholesterol, 194 mg sodium, 11 g carbohydrate, 1 g fiber, 20 g protein*
Daily Value: *0% vitamin A, 5% vitamin C, 1% calcium, 9% iron*

TANGY BARBECUED PORK RIBS

Rich in barbecue flavor, these ribs cook under pressure
in just 12 minutes—a fraction of the time required on the grill or in the oven.

PREPARATION TIME: 10 MINUTES
COOKING TIME: 12 MINUTES

- **3 pounds pork loin back ribs, cut into serving-size pieces**
- **2 cups water**
- **⅓ cup packed brown sugar**
- **1 clove garlic, minced**
- **1 teaspoon dry mustard**
- **¼ teaspoon black pepper**
- **1 8-ounce can tomato sauce**
- **⅓ cup water**
- **3 tablespoons vinegar**

1. Place ribs in a 4- or 6-quart pressure cooker. Add 2 cups water.

2. Lock lid in place. Place pressure regulator on vent pipe (if you have a first-generation cooker). Over high heat, bring cooker up to pressure. Reduce heat just enough to maintain pressure and pressure regulator rocks gently; cook for 5 minutes.

3. Quick-release the pressure. Carefully remove lid. Drain off the liquid.

4. In a medium mixing bowl stir together brown sugar, garlic, mustard, black pepper, tomato sauce, ⅓ cup water, and vinegar. Pour the tomato mixture over the ribs in cooker.

5. Lock lid in place. Place pressure regulator on vent pipe (if you have a first-generation cooker). Over high heat, bring cooker up to pressure. Reduce heat just enough to maintain pressure and pressure regulator rocks gently; cook for 7 minutes.

6. Quick-release the pressure and carefully remove the lid. Makes 4 main-dish servings.

Nutrition facts per serving: *443 calories, 19 g total fat (7 g saturated fat), 95 mg cholesterol, 417 mg sodium, 20 g carbohydrate, 1 g fiber, 46 g protein*
Daily Value: *5% vitamin A, 7% vitamin C, 3% calcium, 17% iron*

STUFFED PORK CHOPS

Pressure cooking makes these chops moist and tender and quick enough for a weekday dinner.

PREPARATION TIME: 20 MINUTES
COOKING TIME: 25 MINUTES

- **4 pork loin rib chops for stuffing, 1¼ inches thick (about 2 pounds)**
- **2 tablespoons cooking oil**
- **1½ cups soft bread crumbs (2 slices)**
- **1 medium apple, peeled and chopped**
- **¼ cup chopped celery**
- **1 tablespoon chopped green onion**
- **1 teaspoon dried sage, crushed**
- **⅛ teaspoon black pepper**
- **½ cup water**

1. Trim any visible fat from meat. Set aside. Cut a pocket in each chop by cutting from fat side almost to bone.

2. In a 4- or 6-quart pressure cooker heat 1 tablespoon of the oil over medium heat. Cook meat, half at a time, till brown on all sides. Add more oil, if needed. Remove the meat and set aside. Drain off fat.

3. For stuffing, in a medium mixing bowl stir together the bread crumbs, apple, celery, green onion, sage, and black pepper. Spoon one-fourth of the stuffing into each chop. Secure pockets with wooden toothpicks.

4. Place rack into pressure cooker. Add the water. Season chops with salt and pepper. Place meat on rack.

5. Lock lid in place. Place pressure regulator on vent pipe (if you have a first-generation cooker). Over high heat, bring cooker up to pressure. Reduce heat just enough to maintain pressure and pressure regulator rocks gently; cook for 15 minutes.

6. Allow pressure to come down naturally. Carefully remove lid.

7. Remove toothpicks before serving. Makes 4 main-dish servings.

Nutrition facts per serving: 291 calories, 14 g total fat (4 g saturated fat), 77 mg cholesterol, 191 mg sodium, 14 g carbohydrate, 1 g fiber, 26 g protein
Daily Value: *0% vitamin A, 5% vitamin C, 3% calcium, 10% iron*

GLAZED MEATBALLS

If you prefer, substitute ground beef for the pork. You can also replace the ham with ground lamb.

PREPARATION TIME: 20 MINUTES
COOKING TIME: 25 MINUTES

1 **egg beaten**
¼ **cup fine dry bread crumbs**
2 **tablespoons finely chopped onion**
¼ **teaspoon salt**
¼ **teaspoon black pepper**
2 **tablespoons milk**
1 **tablespoon prepared mustard**
2 **teaspoons Worcestershire sauce**
1 **teaspoon prepared horseradish**
½ **pound ground pork**
½ **pound ground fully cooked ham**
1 **cup water**
⅓ **cup pineapple preserves or orange marmalade**
¼ **teaspoon dry mustard**

1. In a large mixing bowl stir together the egg, bread crumbs, onion, salt, black pepper, milk, prepared mustard, Worcestershire sauce, and horseradish. Add ground pork and ham and mix till well combined. Divide the meat mixture into four large meatballs.

2. Place rack in a 4- or 6-quart pressure cooker. Add water. Place meatballs on rack.

3. Lock lid in place. Place pressure regulator on vent pipe (if you have a first-generation cooker). Over high heat, bring cooker up to pressure. Reduce heat just enough to maintain pressure and pressure regulator rocks gently; cook for 25 minutes.

4. Allow pressure to come down naturally. Carefully remove lid.

5. Carefully remove meatballs; keep warm. Reserve 2 tablespoons of the cooking liquid for the sauce. In a small saucepan stir together pineapple preserves or orange marmalade and dry mustard. Heat over medium heat till preserves are melted. Stir in reserved cooking liquid and drizzle over meatballs. Makes 4 main-dish servings.

Nutrition facts per serving: 233 calories, 11 g total fat (4 g saturated fat), 121 mg cholesterol, 998 mg sodium, 7 g carbohydrate, 0 g fiber, 25 g protein
Daily Value: 3% vitamin A, 28% vitamin C, 3% calcium, 14% iron

POT ROAST WITH VEGETABLES

The pressure cooker quickly tenderizes round steak for this herb-seasoned pot roast.
Add a tossed salad and French rolls for a meal that's a snap.

PREPARATION TIME: 30 MINUTES
COOKING TIME: 20 MINUTES

1 **pound beef round steak, ½ inch thick**
2 **tablespoons cooking oil**
6 **large carrots, cut into 2-inch pieces**
6 **whole tiny new potatoes, halved**
1 **large onion, peeled and cut into wedges**
1 **teaspoon dried rosemary, crushed**
1 **teaspoon dried thyme, crushed**
¼ **teaspoon salt**
⅛ **teaspoon black pepper**
¾ **cup beef broth or beef stock (page 37)**
2 **tablespoons all-purpose flour**
¼ **cup water**

1. Trim any visible fat from the meat. Set aside.

2. In a 4- or 6-quart pressure cooker heat 1 tablespoon of the oil over medium heat. Cook meat till brown on all sides. Add more oil, if needed. Remove the meat and set aside. Drain off fat.

3. Add carrots, potatoes, onion, rosemary, thyme, salt, black pepper, and beef broth or stock.

4. Lock lid in place. Place pressure regulator on vent pipe (if you have a first-generation cooker). Over high heat, bring cooker up to pressure. Reduce heat just enough to maintain pressure and pressure regulator rocks gently; cook for 8 minutes.

5. Quick-release the pressure. Carefully remove lid. With a slotted spoon remove meat and vegetables to a serving platter; keep warm.

6. In a small mixing bowl stir together flour and water. Stir into broth. Cook till thickened and bubbly. Cook and stir for 1 minute more. Serve over meat and vegetables. Makes 4 main-dish servings.

Nutrition facts per serving: *310 calories, 8 g total fat (2 g saturated fat), 72 mg cholesterol, 407 mg sodium, 28 g carbohydrate, 5 g fiber, 31 g protein*
Daily Value: *256% vitamin A, 20% vitamin C, 5% calcium, 30% iron*

BEEF STROGANOFF

*This creamy, rich dish is loaded with mushrooms and herbs and is perfect served
with a side dish of steamed brussels sprouts and julienne carrots.*

PREPARATION TIME: 25 MINUTES
COOKING TIME: 19 MINUTES

1 **pound beef round steak**
2 **tablespoons cooking oil**
1 ½ **cups sliced fresh
    mushrooms (4 ounces)**
¾ **cup chopped onion**
3 **cloves garlic, minced**
½ **teaspoon dried tarragon,
    crushed**
¼ **teaspoon salt**
¼ **teaspoon black pepper**
1 **8-ounce can tomatoes,
    cut up**
½ **cup beef broth or beef
    stock (page 37)**
2 **tablespoons all-purpose
    flour**
½ **cup dairy sour cream**
¼ **cup snipped fresh
    parsley**
2 **cups hot cooked noodles
    (4 ounces uncooked)**

1. Trim visible fat from meat. Cut meat into bite-size strips. Set aside.

2. In a 4- or 6-quart pressure cooker heat 1 tablespoon of the oil over medium heat. Cook meat till brown on all sides. Add more oil, if needed. Remove the meat and set aside. Drain off fat.

3. Return the meat to cooker and add the mushrooms, onion, garlic, tarragon, salt, black pepper, *undrained* tomatoes, and beef broth or stock.

4. Lock lid in place. Place pressure regulator on vent pipe (if you have a first-generation cooker). Over high heat, bring cooker up to pressure. Reduce heat just enough to maintain pressure and pressure regulator rocks gently; cook for 10 minutes.

5. Allow pressure to come down naturally. Carefully remove lid.

6. In a small mixing bowl stir together the flour and sour cream. Stir in 2 tablespoons of cooking liquid from the pressure cooker. Stir till smooth. Slowly add the sour cream mixture to the beef mixture and cook over medium heat till thickened and bubbly. Cook and stir for 1 minute more. Stir in parsley. Serve over cooked noodles. Makes 4 main-dish servings (3⅔ cups).

Nutrition facts per serving: *412 calories, 16 g total fat (6 g saturated fat), 110 mg cholesterol, 397 mg sodium, 31 g carbohydrate, 3 g fiber, 34 g protein*
Daily Value: *12% vitamin A, 29% vitamin C, 7% calcium, 31% iron*

BEEF BRISKET ON FRENCH ROLLS

Leftover beef can be sliced and stored in an airtight container in the freezer for 2 or 3 months.

PREPARATION TIME: 20 MINUTES
COOKING TIME: 45 MINUTES

- **3 pounds beef brisket, 2 to 3 inches thick**
- **2 tablespoon cooking oil**
- **1 large onion, cut into thin wedges**
- **1 small fennel bulb**
- **1 clove garlic, minced**
- **1 tablespoon finely shredded orange peel**
- **3 cups beef broth or 3 cups water plus 1 tablespoon beef bouillon granules**
- **8 slices mozzarella or provolone cheese (4 ounces)**
- **8 individual French-style rolls, split and toasted**

1. Trim any visible fat from the meat. If necessary, cut meat into two equal pieces to fit in the pressure cooker. Set meat aside.

2. In a 4- or 6-quart pressure cooker heat 1 tablespoon of the oil over medium heat. Cook meat, half at a time, till brown on all sides. Add more oil, if needed. Remove the meat and set aside. Drain off fat.

3. Return the meat to the pressure cooker and add onion wedges, fennel bulb, garlic, orange peel, and beef broth or water and bouillon.

4. Lock lid in place. Place pressure regulator on vent pipe (if you have a first-generation cooker). Over high heat, bring cooker up to pressure. Reduce heat just enough to maintain pressure and pressure regulator rocks gently; cook for 35 minutes.

5. Allow pressure to come down naturally. Carefully remove lid.

6. Transfer meat to a cutting board. Cut the brisket on a diagonal into thin slices. With a slotted spoon remove fennel and slice. With a slotted spoon remove onions to a serving platter. Place meat, cheese, onion, and fennel slices on bottoms of French rolls; add tops of rolls. Skim excess fat from the broth. Serve broth in small bowls with sandwiches; dip sandwiches in the broth. Makes 8 main-dish servings.

Nutrition facts per serving: 481 calories, 22 g total fat (8 g saturated fat), 125 mg cholesterol, 688 mg sodium, 23 g carbohydrate, 0 g fiber, 45 g protein
Daily Value: 2% vitamin A, 6% vitamin C, 12% calcium, 31% iron

CORNED BEEF AND CABBAGE

Don't wait for Saint Patrick's Day to serve this Irish favorite.
It's great year-round served with prepared horseradish and mustard.

PREPARATION TIME: 10 MINUTES
COOKING TIME: 52 MINUTES

1   **3-pound corned beef
    brisket**
½   **cup sliced onion
    (1 small)**
1   **bay leaf**
½   **teaspoon whole black
    peppercorns**
3   **cups water**
1   **1½-pound cabbage, cut
    into 6 wedges**

1. Trim any visible fat from the meat. Set aside.

2. Place rack in a 4- to 6-quart pressure cooker. Add the meat, onion, bay leaf, black peppercorns, and water.

3. Lock lid in place. Place pressure regulator on vent pipe (if you have a first-generation cooker). Over high heat, bring cooker up to pressure. Reduce heat just enough to maintain pressure and pressure regulator rocks gently; cook for 50 minutes.

4. Allow pressure to come down naturally. Carefully remove lid. With a slotted spoon remove the meat and onions to a serving platter; set aside.

5. Place the wedges of cabbage in the pressure cooker. Lock lid in place. Place pressure regulator on vent pipe (if you have a first-generation cooker). Over high heat, bring cooker up to pressure. Reduce heat just enough to maintain pressure and pressure regulator rocks gently; cook for 2 minutes.

6. Quick-release the pressure. Carefully remove lid. With a slotted spoon remove the cabbage wedges. Serve with meat and onions. Makes 6 main-dish servings.

Nutrition facts per serving: *255 calories, 17 g total fat (6 g saturated fat), 88 mg cholesterol, 1,039 mg sodium, 7 g carbohydrate, 4 g fiber, 18 g protein*
Daily Value: *1% vitamin A, 69% vitamin C, 3% calcium, 14% iron*

THAI BEEF AND BROCCOLI

A few well-chosen seasonings turn a round steak and broccoli into a spicy Thai-style entrée.

PREPARATION TIME: 10 MINUTES
COOKING TIME: 19 MINUTES

- 1 **pound beef round steak, ½ inch thick**
- 2 **tablespoons cooking oil**
- 1½ **teaspoons finely shredded lemon peel**
- ½ **to 1 teaspoon crushed red pepper**
- ¾ **cup water**
- 2 **tablespoons soy sauce**
- 2 **teaspoons fish sauce (optional)**
- 4 **cups broccoli flowerets**
- 1 **tablespoon cornstarch**
- 2 **tablespoons water**
- 2 **cups hot cooked rice**

1. Trim fat and bone from the meat. Cut meat into 4 portions. Discard bone. Set aside.

2. In a 4- or 6-quart pressure cooker heat 1 tablespoon of the oil over medium heat. Cook meat, half at a time, till brown on all sides. Add more oil, if needed. Remove the meat and set aside. Drain off fat.

3. Return all the meat to cooker and add the lemon peel, crushed red pepper, water, soy sauce, and if desired, fish sauce.

4. Lock lid in place. Place pressure regulator on vent pipe (if you have a first-generation cooker). Over high heat, bring cooker up to pressure. Reduce heat just enough to maintain pressure and pressure regulator rocks gently; cook for 8 minutes.

5. Quick-release the pressure. Carefully remove lid. Transfer meat to a serving platter; keep warm.

6. Add broccoli to cooker. Bring to boiling; reduce heat. Cover loosely (do not lock lid) and cook for 2 to 3 minutes or till broccoli is crisp-tender. Transfer broccoli to serving platter with meat. In a small mixing bowl stir together cornstarch and water. Add to liquid in cooker. Cook and stir till thickened and bubbly. Cook and stir for 2 minutes more. Serve sauce over beef and broccoli. Serve with rice. Makes 4 main-dish servings.

Nutrition facts per serving: *353 calories, 9 g total fat (2 g saturated fat), 72 mg cholesterol, 612 mg sodium, 33 g carbohydrate, 6 g fiber, 34 g protein*
Daily Value: *23% vitamin A, 194% vitamin C, 7% calcium, 33% iron*

SHREDDED BEEF TACOS

Use any leftover meat in a taco salad. Arrange the meat, cheese, and guacamole on a bed of leaf lettuce.
Add some salsa for a quick salad dressing and serve with corn chips.

PREPARATION TIME: 10 MINUTES
COOKING TIME: 45 MINUTES

- **2 pounds boneless beef chuck roast, 2 inches thick**
- **2 tablespoon cooking oil**
- **¾ cup chopped green or red sweet pepper (1 medium)**
- **½ cup chopped onion (1 medium)**
- **2 to 3 cloves garlic, minced**
- **2 dried chipotle peppers, seeded and chopped or 2 jalapeño peppers, seeded and chopped**
- **1 tablespoon chili powder**
- **¾ cup beef broth or beef stock (page 37)**
- **8 8-inch flour tortillas**
  Guacamole (optional)
  Dairy sour cream (optional)
  Shredded cheddar cheese (optional)
  Shredded lettuce (optional)

1. Trim any visible fat from the meat. Set aside.

2. In a 4- or 6-quart pressure cooker heat 1 tablespoon of the oil over medium heat. Cook meat till brown on all sides. Add more oil, if needed. Remove the meat and set aside. Drain off fat.

3. Place the rack in the pressure cooker. Return the meat to cooker and add the sweet pepper, onion, garlic, chipotle or jalapeño peppers, chili powder, and beef broth or stock.

4. Lock lid in place. Place pressure regulator on vent pipe (if you have a first-generation cooker). Over high heat, bring cooker up to pressure. Reduce heat just enough to maintain pressure and pressure regulator rocks gently; cook for 35 minutes.

5. Allow pressure to come down naturally. Carefully remove lid. Meanwhile, heat tortillas according to package directions.

6. Transfer meat to a cutting board. Using the tines of two forks, pull the meat across the grain to form shreds. With a slotted spoon remove the vegetables to a serving platter. Combine with meat.

7. On each tortilla spoon about ½ cup of the meat mixture. If desired, top with guacamole, sour cream, cheese, and lettuce. Roll up tortillas. Makes 8 main-dish servings (4 cups meat mixture).

Nutrition facts per serving: *327 calories, 12 g total fat (4 g saturated fat), 82 mg cholesterol, 310 mg sodium, 22 g carbohydrate, 1 g fiber, 31 g protein*
Daily Value: *13% vitamin A, 28% vitamin C, 5% calcium, 30% iron*

BEEF CHOP SUEY

For Pork Chop Suey, substitute pork shoulder roast for the beef.
For a chow mein version, substitute chow mein noodles for the rice.

PREPARATION TIME: 20 MINUTES
COOKING TIME: 25 MINUTES

 2 **tablespoons cooking oil**
1½ **pounds beef chuck roast,**
     cut into 1-inch pieces
 2 **cups celery, thinly**
     bias-sliced (4 stalks)
1½ **cups fresh mushrooms,**
     halved (4 ounces)
 1 **slice gingerroot,**
     1½ inches long
 ½ **cup water**
 2 **tablespoons cornstarch**
 3 **tablespoons soy sauce**
 2 **cups fresh bean sprouts**
 1 **8-ounce can sliced water**
     chestnuts or bamboo
     shoots, drained
 ¼ **cup sliced green**
     onions (2)
 ¼ **teaspoon black pepper**
 3 **cups hot cooked rice**

1. In a 4- or 6-quart pressure cooker heat 1 tablespoon of the oil over medium heat. Cook meat, half at a time, till brown on all sides. Add more oil, if needed. Remove the meat and set aside. Drain off fat.

2. Return all the meat to cooker and add celery, mushrooms, and gingerroot. Add the water.

3. Lock lid in place. Place pressure regulator on vent pipe (if you have a first-generation cooker). Over high heat, bring cooker up to pressure. Reduce heat just enough to maintain pressure and pressure regulator rocks gently; cook for 12 minutes.

4. Allow pressure to come down naturally. Carefully remove lid. Remove the ginger.

5. In a small mixing bowl stir together the cornstarch and soy sauce. Slowly pour the soy sauce mixture into the meat mixture in the cooker. Cook, uncovered, over medium heat till thickened and bubbly. Cook and stir for 2 minutes longer.

6. Stir in the bean sprouts, water chestnuts or bamboo shoots, green onions, and pepper. Cook and stir for 1 to 2 minutes or till heated through. Serve over cooked rice. Makes 6 main-dish servings (6 cups).

Nutrition facts per serving: *392 calories, 13 g total fat (4 g saturated fat), 82 mg cholesterol, 632 mg sodium, 36 g carbohydrate, 2 g fiber, 32 g protein*
Daily Value: *1% vitamin A, 17% vitamin C, 4% calcium, 36% iron*

BEEF AND PEPPERS

Use a combination of red, green, and yellow sweet peppers in this colorful, perfectly seasoned beef entrée.

PREPARATION TIME: 10 MINUTES
COOKING TIME: 30 MINUTES

¼ cup all-purpose flour
½ teaspoon salt
¼ teaspoon black pepper
1 pound beef chuck roast,
   cut into 1-inch pieces
2 tablespoons cooking oil
1 teaspoon paprika
1 teaspoon dried oregano,
   crushed
½ teaspoon dried thyme,
   crushed
1 bay leaf
½ cup beef broth or beef
   stock (page 37)
2 tablespoons red wine
   vinegar
1 cup tomato, chopped
   (1 large)
4 cups red, green, or
   yellow sweet peppers,
   cut into ¼-inch strips
   (2 large)
2 cups hot cooked rice,
   noodles, mashed
   potatoes, or boiled new
   potatoes

1. In a medium-sized plastic bag combine the flour, salt, and black pepper. Place half of the meat in the bag and seal. Shake till the meat is coated with flour. Remove meat and repeat with remaining meat.

2. In a 4- to 6-quart pressure cooker heat 1 tablespoon of the oil over medium heat. Cook meat, half at a time, till brown on all sides. Add more oil, if needed. Remove meat and set aside. Drain off fat.

3. Return all meat to the pressure cooker and add the paprika, oregano, thyme, bay leaf, beef broth or stock, red wine vinegar, and tomato.

4. Lock lid in place. Place pressure regulator on vent pipe (if you have a first-generation cooker). Over high heat, bring cooker up to pressure. Reduce heat just enough to maintain pressure and pressure regulator rocks gently; cook for 12 minutes.

5. Allow pressure to come down naturally. Carefully remove lid. Remove the bay leaf.

6. Stir in the sweet peppers. Cover loosely (do not lock lid) and cook over medium heat for 6 to 8 minutes or till peppers are tender. Serve with rice, noodles, or potatoes. Makes 4 main-dish servings (4½ cups).

Nutrition facts per serving: 407 calories, 16 g total fat (4 g saturated fat), 82 mg cholesterol, 425 mg sodium, 35 g carbohydrate, 1 g fiber, 31 g protein
Daily Value: 41% vitamin A, 148% vitamin C, 2% calcium, 35% iron

SLOPPY JOES

*Rolled oats thicken this version of a sandwich that's perfect for a kid's birthday party.
Toast the Kaiser rolls in a toaster oven or under the broiler.*

PREPARATION TIME: 12 MINUTES
COOKING TIME: 13 MINUTES

- 2 **pounds lean ground beef**
- 1 **cup chopped onion**
  (1 large)
- ½ **cup chopped green**
  sweet pepper
- 1 **clove garlic, minced**
- ½ **cup regular rolled oats**
- 1 **tablespoon brown sugar**
- 1 **14½-ounce can stewed**
  tomatoes
- ⅓ **cup water**
- 3 **tablespoons prepared**
  mustard
- 2 **tablespoons**
  Worcestershire sauce
- 12 **Kaiser rolls, split and**
  toasted

1. In a 4- or 6-quart pressure cooker cook ground beef, onion, sweet pepper, and garlic over medium heat till meat is browned.

2. Add the oats, brown sugar, *undrained* tomatoes, water, mustard, and Worcestershire sauce.

3. Lock lid in place. Place pressure regulator on vent pipe (if you have a first-generation cooker). Over high heat, bring cooker up to pressure. Reduce heat just enough to maintain pressure and pressure regulator rocks gently; cook for 8 minutes.

4. Quick-release the pressure. Carefully remove lid. For a thicker consistency, return to boiling and simmer, uncovered, till thickened.

5. Spoon ½ cup of the ground beef mixture onto each roll. Makes 12 servings (6 cups of meat).

Nutrition facts per serving: *351 calories, 12 g total fat (4 g saturated fat), 48 mg cholesterol, 513 mg sodium, 38 g carbohydrate, 1 g fiber, 22 g protein*
Daily Value: *2% vitamin A, 21% vitamin C, 6% calcium, 25% iron*

SPAGHETTI SAUCE

Here's a homemade spaghetti sauce you can enjoy any day of the week.
Use Italian sausage for a robust flavor.

PREPARATION TIME: 25 MINUTES
COOKING TIME: 20 MINUTES

½ **pound ground beef**
½ **pound bulk Italian**
   sausage or bulk pork
   sausage
2 **cups sliced fresh**
   mushrooms (6 ounces)
½ **cup chopped onion**
   (1 medium)
½ **cup sliced celery**
   (1 stalk)
2 **cloves garlic, minced**
⅓ **cup snipped fresh**
   parsley
1 **teaspoon sugar**
1 **teaspoon dried oregano,**
   crushed
¼ **teaspoon crushed red**
   pepper
2 **bay leaves**
1 **28-ounce can stewed**
   tomatoes
1 **6-ounce can tomato**
   paste
6 **cups hot cooked**
   spaghetti or fettuccine,
   (12 ounces uncooked)

1. In a 4- or 6- quart pressure cooker cook beef and sausage till brown. Remove meat. Drain off fat.

2. Return meat to the cooker and add the mushrooms, onion, celery, garlic, parsley, sugar, oregano, crushed red pepper, bay leaves, stewed tomatoes, and tomato paste.

3. Lock lid in place. Place pressure regulator on vent pipe (if you have a first-generation cooker). Over high heat, bring cooker up to pressure. Reduce heat just enough to maintain pressure and pressure regulator rocks gently; cook for 10 minutes.

4. Quick-release the pressure. Carefully remove lid.

5. Remove bay leaves. Serve over spaghetti. Makes 6 main-dish servings (6 cups sauce).

Nutrition facts per serving: *475 calories, 13 g total fat (5 g saturated fat), 45 mg cholesterol, 727 mg sodium, 65 g carbohydrate, 3 g fiber, 24 g protein*
Daily Value: *14% vitamin A, 47% vitamin C, 5% calcium, 35% iron*

LAMB AND ARTICHOKES

These tender lamb chops with artichokes and mushrooms seasoned with mint and lemon cook to perfection in just 20 minutes.

PREPARATION TIME: 20 MINUTES
COOKING TIME: 20 MINUTES

- 4 **lamb sirloin chops, ½ inch thick (1½ pounds)**
- 2 **tablespoons cooking oil**
- ½ **teaspoon salt**
- ½ **teaspoon dried mint, crushed**
- ¼ **teaspoon black pepper**
- ½ **cup beef broth or beef stock (page 37)**
- 1 **9-ounce package frozen artichoke hearts**
- 2 **tablespoons all-purpose flour**
- ½ **cup milk**
- ½ **cup sliced fresh mushrooms**
- 1 **tablespoon lemon juice**
- 2 **cups hot cooked noodles (4 ounces uncooked)**
  Lemon wedges

1. Trim any visible fat from the meat. Set aside.

2. In a 4- or 6-quart pressure cooker heat 1 tablespoon of the oil over medium heat. Cook two chops at a time, till brown on all sides. Add more oil, if needed. Drain off fat.

3. Return all the chops to cooker and add the salt, mint, black pepper, and beef broth or stock.

4. Lock lid in place. Place pressure regulator on vent pipe (if you have a first-generation cooker). Over high heat, bring cooker up to pressure. Reduce heat just enough to maintain pressure and pressure regulator rocks gently; cook for 5 minutes.

5. Quick-release the pressure. Carefully remove lid. Add frozen artichoke hearts to cooker. Return to boiling; reduce heat. Cover loosely (do not lock lid) and simmer about 7 minutes or till artichokes are tender.

6. With a slotted spoon remove the meat and artichokes to a serving platter; keep warm. Skim fat from cooking liquid and reserve ½ cup cooking liquid.

7. For gravy, in a small mixing bowl stir together flour and milk. Add flour mixture, ½ cup cooking liquid, and mushrooms to pressure cooker. Cook and stir over medium heat till thickened and bubbly. Cook and stir for 1 minute more. Stir in lemon juice. Serve gravy over chops and artichokes. Serve with cooked noodles. Garnish with lemon wedges. Makes 4 main-dish servings.

Nutrition facts per serving: *325 calories, 15 g total fat (5 g saturated fat), 106 mg cholesterol, 521 mg sodium, 12 g carbohydrate, 3 g fiber, 36 g protein*
Daily Value: *3% vitamin A, 14% vitamin C, 6% calcium, 24% iron*

LAMB AND VEGETABLE ROLL

*Rosemary and thyme season this marvelous rolled lamb roast that cooks
in the pressure cooker in one-third the time it would take in the oven.*

PREPARATION TIME: 20 MINUTES
COOKING TIME: 45 MINUTES

½ **cup fine dry bread
  crumbs**
½ **cup shredded carrot
  (1 medium)**
¼ **cup red or yellow sweet
  pepper cut into thin
  strips (1 small)**
½ **teaspoon dried
  rosemary, crushed**
½ **teaspoon dried thyme,
  crushed**
1 **to 2 tablespoons chicken
  broth or chicken stock
  (page 36)**
1 **3-pound tied boneless
  lamb shoulder roast**
2 **tablespoons cooking oil**
2 **cloves garlic, minced**
2 **cups chicken broth, beef
  broth, chicken stock
  (page 36), or beef stock
  (page 37)**
  Mustard Sauce

1. In a small mixing bowl combine bread crumbs, carrots, sweet pepper, rosemary, and thyme. Stir in 1 to 2 tablespoons of the chicken broth or stock to moisten. Set aside.

2. Untie roast and pound meat with a meat mallet to an even thickness. Spread the bread crumb mixture over the meat. Roll up; tie securely.

3. In a 4- or 6-quart pressure cooker heat 1 tablespoon of the oil over medium heat. Cook meat till brown on all sides. Add more oil, if needed. Remove the meat and set aside. Drain off fat.

4. Return the meat to the pressure cooker. Add the garlic and 2 cups chicken or beef broth or stock.

5. Lock lid in place. Place pressure regulator on vent pipe (if you have a first-generation cooker). Over high heat, bring cooker up to pressure. Reduce heat just enough to maintain pressure and pressure regulator rocks gently; cook for 35 minutes.

6. Allow pressure to come down naturally. Carefully remove lid.

7. Transfer the roast to a serving platter. Slice and serve with Mustard Sauce. Makes 8 main-dish servings.

MUSTARD SAUCE: In a small bowl stir together ¼ cup *dairy sour cream,* ¼ cup *mayonnaise or salad dressing,* 1 tablespoon *Dijon-style mustard,* and, if desired, 1 teaspoon *prepared horseradish.* Makes ½ cup.

Nutrition facts per serving: *315 calories, 17 g total fat (5 g saturated fat), 100 mg cholesterol, 405 mg sodium, 7 g carbohydrate, 1 g fiber, 31 g protein*
Daily Value: *35% vitamin A, 14% vitamin C, 3% calcium, 19% iron*

LAMB WITH FRUIT

*Cooking under pressure is the perfect choice for less tender cuts of lamb,
such as this shoulder roast. The dried fruit sauce enhances the richness of the meat.*

PREPARATION TIME: 10 MINUTES
COOKING TIME: 58 MINUTES

- 1 **3-pound tied boneless lamb shoulder roast**
- ½ **teaspoon salt**
- ¼ **teaspoon black pepper**
- ¼ **teaspoon ground cumin**
- 2 **tablespoons cooking oil**
- 1½ **cups water**
- ¼ **cup dry white wine**
- ½ **cup dried apples**
- ½ **cup dried apricots**
- ½ **cup dried figs**
- 1 **tablespoon lemon juice**
- 4 **cups hot cooked spaetzle or noodles (optional)**

1. Trim any visible fat from the meat. Set aside. In a small mixing bowl stir together salt, black pepper, and cumin; rub over meat.

2. In a 4- or 6-quart pressure cooker heat 1 tablespoon of the oil over medium heat. Cook meat till brown on all sides. Add more oil, if needed. Remove the meat and set aside. Drain off fat.

3. Return meat to the pressure cooker and add the water and wine.

4. Lock lid in place. Place pressure regulator on vent pipe (if you have a first-generation cooker). Over high heat, bring cooker up to pressure. Reduce heat just enough to maintain pressure and pressure regulator rocks gently; cook for 35 minutes.

5. Allow pressure to come down naturally. Carefully remove lid. Transfer meat to serving platter; keep warm.

6. Skim fat from pan juices. Bring to boiling. Boil about 5 minutes or till juices are reduced to 1½ cups. Add the dried apples, apricots, and figs. Simmer, uncovered, for 6 to 8 minutes longer or till fruit is tender and mixture is slightly thickened. Stir in the lemon juice. Slice meat and serve with the fruit sauce. If desired, serve with spaetzle or noodles. Makes 6 main-dish servings.

Nutrition facts per serving: *325 calories, 11 g total fat (3 g saturated fat), 103 mg cholesterol, 276 mg sodium, 23 g carbohydrate, 3 g fiber, 33 g protein*
Daily Value: *8% vitamin A, 3% vitamin C, 4% calcium, 25% iron*

VEGETARIAN HOPPIN' JOHN

In the South, Hoppin' John is served on New Year's Day to ensure good luck for the year. Our meatless version of this traditional recipe omits the bacon or salt pork and adds tomatoes and fresh spinach for additional flavor.

PREPARATION TIME: 10 MINUTES
COOKING TIME: 10 MINUTES

1½ **cups dry black-eyed peas, rinsed and drained**
1½ **cups coarsely chopped onions (3 medium)**
1 **clove garlic, minced**
2½ **cups water**
2 **tablespoons cooking oil**
1½ **cups tightly packed, chopped fresh spinach**
¾ **teaspoon salt**
1 **14½-ounce can tomatoes, cut up**
¼ **teaspoon bottled hot pepper sauce**
3 **cups hot cooked rice**

1. In a 4- or 6-quart pressure cooker combine the black-eyed peas, onions, garlic, water, and oil.

2. Lock lid in place. Place pressure regulator on vent pipe (if you have a first-generation cooker). Over high heat, bring cooker up to pressure. Reduce heat just enough to maintain pressure and pressure regulator rocks gently; cook for 8 minutes.

3. Quick-release the pressure. Carefully remove lid.

4. Stir in the spinach, salt, *undrained* tomatoes, and hot pepper sauce. Heat through. Stir in the hot cooked rice. Serve with additional hot pepper sauce, if desired. Makes 4 main-dish servings (7 cups).

Nutrition facts per serving: 430 calories, 8 g total fat (1 g saturated fat), 0 mg cholesterol, 599 mg sodium, 79 g carbohydrate, 13 g fiber, 11 g protein
Daily Value: 33% vitamin A, 48% vitamin C, 24% calcium, 31% iron

LENTILS WITH BROWN RICE AND BEAN SPROUTS

*Lentils bring their special peppery taste while bean sprouts add crunch
to this one-dish meal of nutty brown rice and vegetables.*

PREPARATION TIME: 35 MINUTES
COOKING TIME: 8 MINUTES

- 1 **cup dry lentils, rinsed and drained**
- 1½ **cups diced carrots (3 medium)**
- 1 **cup coarsely chopped onion (1 large)**
- 1 **cup sliced celery (2 stalks)**
- 3 **cloves garlic, minced**
- ½ **teaspoon salt**
- ⅛ **teaspoon black pepper**
- 1 **14½-ounce can vegetable broth**
- 2 **tablespoons margarine**
- 3 **cups cooked brown rice**
- 1 **cup fresh bean sprouts**
- ¼ **cup snipped fresh parsley**

1. In a 4- or 6-quart pressure cooker combine the lentils, carrots, onion, celery, garlic, salt, black pepper, vegetable broth, and margarine.

2. Lock lid in place. Place pressure regulator on vent pipe (if you have a first-generation cooker). Over high heat, bring cooker up to pressure. Reduce heat just enough to maintain pressure and pressure regulator rocks gently; cook for 5 minutes.

3. Quick-release the pressure. Carefully remove lid.

4. Stir in the cooked rice, bean sprouts, and parsley. Heat through. Makes 4 main-dish servings (7 cups).

Nutrition facts per serving: 454 calories, 8 g total fat (4 g saturated fat), 15 mg cholesterol, 821 mg sodium, 81 g carbohydrate, 8 g fiber, 20 g protein
Daily Value: 136% vitamin A, 28% vitamin C, 8% calcium, 47% iron

Typically, lentils are a tiny brownish-green, disk-shaped, dried seed that is a member of the legume family. Lentils are a source of vegetable protein. Cooked lentils have a beanlike texture and a mild, nutty flavor. Yellow varieties and red (actually orange in color) varieties of lentils are also available.

SAVORY GRAINS AND VEGETABLES

This pilaflike dish is made with bulgur and quinoa (pronounced KEEN-wah) instead of rice.
Look for these grains in a health food store.

PREPARATION TIME: 15 MINUTES
COOKING TIME: 2 MINUTES

- **2 cups sliced carrots (4 medium)**
- **1 cup coarsely chopped onion (1 large)**
- **1 cup sliced celery (2 stalks)**
- **½ cup raisins, light raisins, or dried apple pieces**
- **1 teaspoon dried oregano, crushed**
- **2 cloves garlic, minced**
- **¼ teaspoon curry powder**
- **⅛ teaspoon black pepper**
- **1¼ cups vegetable broth or vegetable stock (page 35)**
- **1½ cups cooked quinoa**
- **½ cup bulgur**
- **¼ cup sliced almonds, toasted**
- **3 tablespoons snipped fresh parsley**

1. In a 4- or 6-quart pressure cooker combine the carrots, onion, celery, raisins, oregano, garlic, curry powder, black pepper, and vegetable broth or stock.

2. Lock lid in place. Place pressure regulator on vent pipe (if you have a first-generation cooker). Over high heat, bring cooker up to pressure. Reduce heat just enough to maintain pressure and pressure regulator rocks gently; cook for 2 minutes.

3. Quick-release the pressure. Carefully remove lid.

4. Stir in the cooked quinoa and bulgur. Cover loosely (do not lock the lid) and let stand about 5 minutes. Stir in the almonds and parsley. Makes 4 main-dish servings (6 cups).

Nutrition facts per serving: 303 calories, 6 g total fat (1 g saturated fat), 0 mg cholesterol, 392 mg sodium, 61 g carbohydrate, 10 g fiber, 9 g protein
Daily Value: 173% vitamin A, 19% vitamin C, 9% calcium, 28% iron

Red Beans and Potatoes

*Chunks of potato cooked with tomato sauce, green chilies, cumin,
and red pepper are combined with red kidney beans for a spicy vegetable stew.*

Preparation Time: soaking time for
beans plus 20 minutes
Cooking Time: 13 minutes

- **1 cup dry red kidney beans**
- **3 cups water**
- **2 tablespoons cooking oil**
- **3 medium potatoes, peeled and cut into ¾-inch cubes**
- **4 cloves garlic, minced**
- **½ teaspoon ground cumin**
- **¼ teaspoon salt**
- **⅛ teaspoon ground red pepper**
- **1 8-ounce can tomato sauce**
- **1 4½-ounce can chopped green chili peppers**
- **½ cup water**
- **1 tablespoon red wine vinegar**
- **3 flour tortillas, warmed, or pita breads**

1. Rinse beans. In a large saucepan combine beans and enough water to cover. Bring to boiling; reduce heat. Simmer for 2 minutes. Remove from heat. Cover and let stand 1 hour. (Or, omit boiling and soak beans overnight.)

2. Drain and rinse the beans. In a 4- or 6-quart pressure cooker combine beans, 3 cups water, and oil. Lock lid in place. Place pressure regulator on vent pipe (if you have a first-generation cooker). Over high heat, bring cooker up to pressure. Reduce heat just enough to maintain pressure and pressure regulator rocks gently; cook for 8 minutes.

3. Quick-release the pressure. Carefully remove lid. Drain beans and set aside.

4. In pressure cooker combine the potatoes, garlic, cumin, salt, ground red pepper, tomato sauce, green chili peppers, ½ cup water, and vinegar.

5. Close cover securely. Place pressure regulator on vent pipe (if you have a first-generation cooker). Over high heat, bring cooker up to pressure with pressure regulator rocking slowly and cook for 3 minutes

6. Quick-release the pressure. Carefully remove lid. Stir in beans and heat through. Meanwhile, wrap flour tortillas in foil and heat in a 350° oven for 10 minutes. Serve with flour tortillas or pita bread. Makes 3 main-dish servings (4 cups).

Nutrition facts per serving: 640 calories, 12 g total fat (2 g saturated fat), 0 mg cholesterol, 1182 mg sodium, 114 g carbohydrate, 6 g fiber, 24 g protein
Daily Value: 7% vitamin A, 59% vitamin C, 16% calcium, 52% iron

RATATOUILLE WITH WHITE BEANS

*With the addition of small navy beans, this classic French vegetable stew is transformed
into a hearty main dish. Enjoy it piping hot, accompanied by a loaf of crusty bread.*

PREPARATION TIME: SOAKING TIME FOR
BEANS PLUS 15 MINUTES
COOKING TIME: 18 MINUTES

1 cup dry navy (pea)
   beans
2 cups coarsely chopped
   onions (2 large)
3 cloves garlic, minced
2 teaspoons dried basil,
   crushed
1 teaspoon dried oregano,
   crushed
¾ teaspoon salt
¼ teaspoon black pepper
2 cups water
2 tablespoons olive oil or
   cooking oil
4 cups eggplant, peeled
   and cut into 1-inch
   cubes (1 medium)
2 cups zucchini, halved
   lengthwise and cut into
   ½-inch slices (1 large)
¾ cup chopped red sweet
   pepper (1 medium)
1 28-ounce can tomatoes,
   cut up

1. Rinse beans. In a large saucepan combine beans and enough water
to cover them. Bring to boiling; reduce heat. Simmer for 2 minutes.
Remove from heat. Cover and let stand 1 hour. (Or, omit boiling and
soak beans overnight.)

2. Drain and rinse the beans. In a 4- or 6-quart pressure cooker
combine the beans, onions, garlic, basil, oregano, salt, black pepper,
water, and oil.

3. Lock lid in place. Place pressure regulator on vent pipe (if you have a
first-generation cooker). Over high heat, bring cooker up to pressure.
Reduce heat just enough to maintain pressure and pressure regulator
rocks gently; cook for 8 minutes.

4. Quick-release pressure. Carefully remove lid.

5. Add the eggplant, zucchini, sweet pepper, and *undrained* tomatoes
to cooker. Bring to boiling; reduce heat. Cover loosely (do not lock lid)
and cook for 5 to 8 minutes or till vegetables are tender. Makes 5 main-
dish servings (10 cups).

Nutrition facts per serving: 264 calories, 7 g total fat (1 g saturated fat), 0 mg cholesterol,
588 mg sodium, 44 g carbohydrate, 5 g fiber, 11 g protein
Daily Value: 21% vitamin A, 94% vitamin C, 11% calcium, 26% iron

CURRIED GARBANZO BEANS WITH CAULIFLOWER

Garlic, gingerroot, cumin, and cilantro blend with curry powder to give the plump garbanzo beans and tender cauliflower a spicy Indian flavor. Serve the curry with wedges of warm pita bread.

PREPARATION TIME: SOAKING TIME FOR BEANS PLUS 10 MINUTES
COOKING TIME: 18 MINUTES

- 1 **cup dry garbanzo beans**
- ⅔ **cup chopped onion**
- 1 **large clove garlic, minced**
- 2 **cups water**
- 2 **tablespoons cooking oil**
- 2 **cups cauliflower flowerets**
- 1½ **teaspoons curry powder**
- ¾ **teaspoon grated gingerroot**
- ½ **teaspoon salt**
- ½ **teaspoon ground cumin**
- ¼ **teaspoon dry mustard**
- 1 **14½-ounce can tomatoes, cut up**
- 1 **tablespoon snipped fresh cilantro**

1. Rinse beans. In a large saucepan combine beans and enough water to cover them. Bring to boiling; reduce heat. Simmer for 2 minutes. Remove from heat. Cover and let stand 1 hour. (Or, omit boiling and soak beans overnight.)

2. Drain and rinse the beans. In a 4- or 6-quart pressure cooker combine the beans, onion, garlic, water, and oil.

3. Lock lid in place. Place pressure regulator on vent pipe (if you have a first-generation cooker). Over high heat, bring cooker up to pressure. Reduce heat just enough to maintain pressure and pressure regulator rocks gently; cook for 8 minutes.

4. Quick-release the pressure. Carefully remove lid. Drain beans. Return the beans to the pressure cooker.

5. Add the cauliflower, curry powder, gingerroot, salt, cumin, mustard, and *undrained* tomatoes. Bring to boiling; reduce heat. Cover loosely (do not lock lid) and cook for 8 to 10 minutes or till cauliflower is tender. Stir in cilantro. Makes 4 main-dish servings (4½ cups).

Nutrition facts per serving: 289 calories, 10 g total fat (1 g saturated fat), 0 mg cholesterol, 459 mg sodium, 41 g carbohydrate, 1 g fiber, 13 g protein
Daily Value: 6% vitamin A, 63% vitamin C, 10% calcium, 31% iron

BLACK BEAN AND COUSCOUS PICADILLO

*This tiny grainlike pasta from North Africa is precooked and only requires
soaking in hot liquid for 5 minutes before serving.*

PREPARATION TIME: SOAKING TIME FOR
BEANS PLUS 15 MINUTES
COOKING TIME: 8 MINUTES

1½ cups dry black beans
1½ cups coarsely chopped
    onions (3 medium)
½ cup raisins
3 cloves garlic, minced
1 to 2 jalapeño peppers,
    seeded and finely
    chopped
1 teaspoon ground
    cinnamon
½ teaspoon salt
¼ teaspoon ground cloves
2 cups water
1 tablespoon cooking oil
1 28-ounce can tomatoes,
    cut up
⅔ cup couscous
⅓ cup sliced pimiento-
    stuffed green olives
⅓ cup slivered almonds,
    toasted
12 flour tortillas, warmed

1. Rinse beans. In a large saucepan combine beans and enough water to cover. Bring to boiling, reduce heat. Simmer for 2 minutes. Remove from heat. Cover and let stand 1 hour. (Or, omit boiling and soak beans overnight.)

2. Drain and rinse the beans. In a 4- or 6-quart pressure cooker combine the beans, onions, raisins, garlic, jalapeño peppers, cinnamon, salt, cloves, water, and oil.

3. Lock lid in place. Place pressure regulator on vent pipe (if you have a first-generation cooker). Over high heat, bring cooker up to pressure. Reduce heat just enough to maintain pressure and pressure regulator rocks gently; cook for 6 minutes.

4. Quick-release the pressure. Carefully remove lid.

5. Stir in *undrained* tomatoes; bring to boiling. Remove from heat. Stir in couscous and olives. Cover loosely (do not lock lid) and let stand 5 minutes. Stir in almonds. Meanwhile, wrap flour tortillas in foil and heat in a 350° oven for 10 minutes.

6. Serve the picadillo with the warm tortillas. Makes 6 main-dish servings (9¾ cups).

*Nutrition facts per serving: 598 calories, 13 g total fat (2 g saturated fat), 0 mg cholesterol,
884 mg sodium, 103 g carbohydrate, 8 g fiber, 22 g protein*
Daily Value: 8% vitamin A, 51% vitamin C, 17% calcium, 43% iron

SPANISH-STYLE PINTOS

For a special treat to serve with these spicy beans, warm tortilla chips in a 350° oven for 5 minutes.

PREPARATION TIME: SOAKING TIME FOR
BEANS PLUS 12 MINUTES
COOKING TIME: 20 MINUTES

1½ **cups dry pinto beans**
1 **cup chopped onion**
    (1 large)
1 **cup sliced celery**
    (2 stalks)
3 **cups water**
2 **tablespoons olive oil or**
    cooking oil
1 **cup chopped green**
    sweet pepper (1 large)
2 **teaspoons chili powder**
¼ **teaspoon dry mustard**
¼ **to ½ teaspoon crushed**
    red pepper
¼ **teaspoon salt**
1 **14½-ounce can tomatoes,**
    cut up
1 **8-ounce can tomato**
    sauce
    Dairy sour cream
    (optional)
    Sliced ripe olives
    (optional)
    Shredded cheddar
    cheese (optional)

1. Rinse beans. In a large saucepan combine beans and enough water to cover them. Bring to boiling; reduce heat. Simmer for 2 minutes. Remove from heat. Cover and let stand 1 hour. (Or, omit boiling and soak beans overnight.)

2. Drain and rinse the beans. In a 4- or 6-quart pressure cooker combine the beans, onion, celery, water, and oil.

3. Lock lid in place. Place pressure regulator on vent pipe (if you have a first-generation cooker). Over high heat, bring cooker up to pressure. Reduce heat just enough to maintain pressure and pressure regulator rocks gently; cook for 8 minutes.

4. Quick-release the pressure. Carefully remove lid. Drain beans. Return the beans to the pressure cooker.

5. Stir in the sweet pepper, chili powder, dry mustard, crushed red pepper, salt, *undrained* tomatoes, and tomato sauce. Bring to boiling. Simmer, uncovered, about 10 minutes. If desired, serve with sour cream, sliced olives, and cheese. Makes 6 main-dish servings (6 cups).

Nutrition facts per serving: 228 calories, 6 g total fat (1 g saturated fat), 0 mg cholesterol, 473 mg sodium, 37 g carbohydrate, 6 g fiber, 10 g protein
Daily Value: 12% vitamin A, 51% vitamin C, 8% calcium, 25% iron

White Bean and Basil Salad

Use large white beans, such as great northern or cannellini (white kidney), for this special main-dish salad. It is fragrant with fresh basil, garlic, and Parmesan cheese.

Preparation Time: soaking time for beans plus 20 minutes
Cooking Time: 8 minutes

- 2 cups dry great northern or cannellini beans
- 1 cup coarsely chopped onion (1 large)
- 2 cloves garlic, minced
- ⅛ teaspoon black pepper
- 2½ cups water
- 2 tablespoons olive oil or cooking oil
- 1 tablespoon snipped fresh basil or 1 teaspoon dried basil, crushed
- ½ teaspoon salt
- ⅓ cup vinegar
- 2 tablespoons olive oil or cooking oil
- 2 cups quartered cherry tomatoes
- 1⅓ cups chopped zucchini (1 medium)
- 2 tablespoons freshly shredded Parmesan cheese (1 ounce)

1. Rinse beans. In a large saucepan combine beans and enough water to cover them. Bring to boiling; reduce heat. Simmer for 2 minutes. Remove from heat. Cover and let stand 1 hour. (Or, omit boiling and soak beans overnight.)

2. Drain and rinse the beans. In a 4- or 6-quart pressure cooker combine beans, onion, garlic, black pepper, water, and 2 tablespoons oil.

3. Lock lid in place. Place pressure regulator on vent pipe (if you have a first-generation cooker). Over high heat, bring cooker up to pressure. Reduce heat just enough to maintain pressure and pressure regulator rocks gently; cook for 8 minutes.

4. Quick-release the pressure. Carefully remove lid. Drain beans. Return beans to pressure cooker.

5. Stir in the basil, salt, vinegar, and 2 tablespoons oil. Serve warm or cool to room temperature. Toss with tomatoes, zucchini, and cheese before serving. Makes 6 main-dish servings (8 cups).

Nutrition facts per serving: 319 calories, 11 g total fat (1 g saturated fat), 2 mg cholesterol, 217 mg sodium, 45 g carbohydrate, 2 g fiber, 14 g protein
Daily Value: 5% vitamin A, 33% vitamin C, 11% calcium, 27% iron

CHUNKY VEGETABLE COUSCOUS

*This attractive main dish is made with a colorful assortment of
seven different vegetables and tossed with fluffy couscous.*

PREPARATION TIME: 25 MINUTES
COOKING TIME: 1 MINUTE

- **2 cups thinly sliced leeks (6)**
- **1½ cups carrots, halved lengthwise and cut into ¼-inch slices (3 medium)**
- **1⅓ cups yellow summer squash, quartered lengthwise and cut into 1-inch slices (1 medium)**
- **1⅓ cups fresh green beans, trimmed and cut into ½-inch pieces (8 ounces)**
- **1 cup red sweet pepper, cut into ¼-inch strips (1 medium)**
- **1 cup sliced celery (2 stalks)**
- **¾ teaspoon dried thyme, crushed**
- **½ teaspoon salt**
- **¼ teaspoon black pepper**
- **2 cups water**
- **1 tablespoon margarine or butter**
- **1½ cups couscous**
- **½ cup frozen peas**

1. In a 4- or 6-quart pressure cooker combine the leeks, carrots, squash, beans, sweet pepper, celery, thyme, salt, black pepper, water, and margarine or butter.

2. Lock lid in place. Place pressure regulator on vent pipe (if you have a first-generation cooker). Over high heat, bring cooker up to pressure. Reduce heat just enough to maintain pressure and pressure regulator rocks gently; cook for 1 minute.

3. Quick-release the pressure. Carefully remove lid.

4. Stir in the couscous and peas. Cover and let stand about 5 minutes. Makes 5 main-dish servings (about 8 cups).

Nutrition facts per serving: 378 calories, 3 g total fat (1 g saturated fat), 0 mg cholesterol, 352 mg sodium, 77 g carbohydrate, 16 g fiber, 12 g protein
Daily Value: 122% vitamin A, 87% vitamin C, 13% calcium, 34% iron

EGGPLANT AND MUSHROOM PASTA SAUCE

*This chunky pasta sauce, flavored with garlic and herbs,
cooks in just 2 minutes but has a deliciously rich, slow-simmered taste.*

PREPARATION TIME: 20 MINUTES
COOKING TIME: 2 MINUTES

4 cups eggplant, peeled
   and cut into 1-inch
   cubes (1 medium)
2 cups quartered fresh
   mushrooms (5 ounces)
1 cup coarsely chopped
   onion (1 large)
2 cloves garlic, minced
1 teaspoon salt
1 teaspoon dried basil,
   crushed
½ teaspoon dried oregano,
   crushed
½ teaspoon dried thyme,
   crushed
¼ teaspoon black pepper
1 bay leaf
1 28-ounce can tomatoes,
   cut up
1 12-ounce can tomato
   paste
½ cup water
4 cups hot cooked
   corkscrew macaroni
   (about 6 ounces
   uncooked)
⅓ cup grated Parmesan
   cheese

1. In a 4- or 6-quart pressure cooker combine the eggplant, mushrooms, onion, garlic, salt, basil, oregano, thyme, black pepper, bay leaf, *undrained* tomatoes, tomato paste, and water.

2. Lock lid in place. Place pressure regulator on vent pipe (if you have a first-generation cooker). Over high heat, bring cooker up to pressure. Reduce heat just enough to maintain pressure and pressure regulator rocks gently; cook for 2 minutes.

3. Quick-release the pressure. Carefully remove lid. Serve over hot cooked pasta and sprinkle with cheese. Makes 6 main-dish servings (about 8 cups).

Nutrition facts per serving: 271 calories, 3 g total fat (1 g saturated fat), 4 mg cholesterol, 717 mg sodium, 52 g carbohydrate, 8 g fiber, 12 g protein
Daily Value: *23% vitamin A, 80% vitamin C, 13% calcium, 34% iron*

Fresh eggplant is available year-round. Look for plum, glossy, heavy eggplant. Skip any with scarred, bruised, or dull surfaces. The cap should be fresh-looking, tight, and free of mold. Refrigerate whole eggplant for up to 2 days.

SAVORY GARDEN VEGETABLES WITH GOUDA

This attractive medley of vegetables is seasoned with savory and ready to eat in the time it takes the pressure cooker to reach pressure. Top each serving with shreds of smoky-flavored Gouda cheese.

PREPARATION TIME: 20 MINUTES
COOKING TIME: 0 MINUTES

- ¾ cup water
- 2 cups quartered fresh mushrooms
- 2 cups broccoli flowerets
- 1⅓ cups zucchini, cut into ½-inch slices (1 medium)
- 1½ cups red sweet pepper, cut into bite-size strips (1 large)
- ½ cup green onions, cut into ½-inch pieces (4)
- 1 tablespoon margarine or butter
- 1 teaspoon dried savory, crushed
- ½ teaspoon salt
- ⅛ teaspoon black pepper
- ½ cup shredded Gouda cheese (2 ounces)

1. Place rack in a 4- or 6-quart pressure cooker and add the water.

2. Place the mushrooms, broccoli, zucchini, sweet pepper, and green onions on rack. Dot with margarine and sprinkle with savory, salt, and black pepper.

3. Lock lid in place. Place pressure regulator on vent pipe (if you have a first-generation cooker). Over high heat, bring cooker up to pressure and cook till pressure regulator begins to rock slowly.

4. Quick-release the pressure. Carefully remove lid. With a slotted spoon remove the vegetables to serving dishes and sprinkle each serving with cheese. Makes 6 side-dish servings (4 cups).

Nutrition facts per serving: 122 calories, 8 g total fat (4 g saturated fat), 24 mg cholesterol, 387 mg sodium, 6 g carbohydrate, 3 g fiber, 8 g protein
Daily Value: 27% vitamin A, 116% vitamin C, 15% calcium, 8% iron

POTATOES AND CARROTS AUGRATIN

Sour cream and sharp cheddar will make this a favorite potato dish at your dinner table.
For an easy transformation to an entrée, just add diced cooked ham, chicken, or beef.

PREPARATION TIME: 30 MINUTES
COOKING TIME: 5 MINUTES

- 3 **cups potatoes, peeled and cut into ¼-inch slices (4 medium)**
- 2 **cups carrots, thinly sliced**
- 1 **cup red sweet pepper, cut into ¼-inch wide strips (1 medium)**
- ½ **teaspoon garlic salt**
- 1 **cup water**
- 1 **tablespoon cooking oil**
- 1 **cup shredded cheddar cheese (4 ounces)**
- ½ **cup sliced green onions (4)**
- ½ **cup dairy sour cream**
- ½ **of an 8-ounce container soft-style cream cheese**
- 3 **tablespoons milk**
  Paprika

1. In a 4- or 6-quart pressure cooker place the potatoes. Top with the carrots and sweet pepper. Add the garlic salt, water, and oil.

2. Lock lid in place. Place pressure regulator on vent pipe (if you have a first-generation cooker). Over high heat, bring cooker up to pressure. Reduce heat just enough to maintain pressure and pressure regulator rocks gently; remove the vegetables.

3. In the pressure cooker stir together the cheddar cheese, green onions, sour cream, cream cheese, and milk. Cook over low heat till heated through and cheddar cheese is melted. Stir in vegetables to coat. Sprinkle with paprika. Makes 10 side-dish servings (about 6 cups).

Nutrition facts per serving: 186 calories, 12 g total fat (6 g saturated fat), 30 mg cholesterol, 235 mg sodium, 15 g carbohydrate, 1 g fiber, 5 g protein
Daily Value: 49% vitamin A, 30% vitamin C, 9% calcium, 2% iron

GERMAN POTATO SALAD

*The pressure cooker cooks the potatoes for this sweet and tangy bacon-flavored salad in almost no time at all.
Use the pressure cooker to make short work of cooking potatoes for any of your other favorite potato dishes.*

PREPARATION TIME: 15 MINUTES
COOKING TIME: 12 MINUTES

6 **slices bacon, diced**
2 **tablespoons all-purpose**
   flour
5½ **cups red potatoes,**
   quartered and cut
   into ¼-inch slices
   (6 medium)
½ **cup chopped onion**
   (1 medium)
1 **cup water**
2 **tablespoons sugar**
1 **teaspoon celery seed**
¾ **teaspoon salt**
⅛ **teaspoon black pepper**
¼ **cup vinegar**
1 **tablespoon snipped**
   fresh parsley

1. In a 4- or 6-quart pressure cooker cook the bacon till crisp over medium heat. Remove pressure cooker from heat. With slotted spoon remove bacon and drain on paper towels.

2. Stir together 2 tablespoons of the bacon drippings with the flour; set aside. Discard remaining drippings.

3. Add the potatoes, onion, and water to the pressure cooker. Lock lid in place. Place pressure regulator on vent pipe (if you have a first-generation cooker). Over high heat, bring cooker up to pressure and cook till pressure regulator begins to rock slowly.

4. Quick-release the pressure. Carefully remove lid.

5. With a slotted spoon remove the potatoes and onion to a large bowl and sprinkle with the bacon. Measure the cooking liquid. (If necessary, add additional water to make 1 cup.) Return 1 cup cooking liquid to pressure cooker.

6. Stir the flour-drippings mixture into the cooking liquid. Add the sugar, celery seed, salt, black pepper, and vinegar. Cook and stir till thickened and bubbly over medium-high heat. Cook and stir for 1 minute more. Pour over the potatoes and toss gently to combine. Sprinkle with parsley. Serve warm. Makes 8 to 10 side-dish servings (7 cups).

Nutrition facts per serving: 161 calories, 3 g total fat (1 g saturated fat), 4 mg cholesterol, 286 mg sodium, 31 g carbohydrate, 1 g fiber, 4 g protein
Daily Value: 0% vitamin A, 29% vitamin C, 2% calcium, 15% iron

LEMONY PARSNIPS

The sweet nutty taste of parsnips is enhanced with the addition of fine shreds of fresh lemon peel
plus a little butter, sugar, and lemon juice. For variety, substitute carrots for half or all of the parsnips.

PREPARATION TIME: 8 MINUTES
COOKING TIME: 1 MINUTE

3½ **cups parsnips, peeled
and cut into ½-inch
slices (about 1 pound)**
1 **tablespoon sugar**
1 **tablespoon lemon juice**
½ **cup water**
½ **teaspoon finely
shredded lemon peel**
¼ **teaspoon salt
Dash of black pepper**
1 **tablespoon margarine or
butter**
1 **tablespoon snipped
fresh parsley**

1. In a 4- or 6-quart pressure cooker combine the parsnips, sugar, water, and lemon juice.

2. Lock lid in place. Place pressure regulator on vent pipe (if you have a first-generation cooker). Over high heat, bring cooker up to pressure. Reduce heat just enough to maintain pressure and pressure regulator rocks gently; cook for 1 minute.

3. Quick-release pressure. Carefully remove lid.

4. With a slotted spoon remove parsnips to a serving bowl. Stir the margarine, lemon peel, salt, black pepper, and margarine into the parsnips. Sprinkle with parsley. Makes 6 side-dish servings (3½ cups).

Nutrition facts per serving: 89 calories, 2 g total fat (0 g saturated fat), 0 mg cholesterol, 120 mg sodium, 18 g carbohydrate, 4 g fiber, 1 g protein
Daily Value: 2% vitamin A, 20% vitamin C, 2% calcium, 3% iron

Fresh parsnips are available year-round, with peak season during January, February, and March. Look for small to medium parsnips that are firm with fairly smooth skin and few rootlets. Avoid shriveled, limp, or cracked parsnips.

SPICED CARROT RELISH

These quick-to-fix pickled carrot slices make a tangy, attractive accompaniment for pork, chicken, or smoked ham entrees. For special occasions, julienne the carrots instead of slicing them.

PREPARATION TIME: 15 MINUTES
COOKING TIME: 2 MINUTES

- **3 cups carrots, sliced ¼-inch thick (6 medium)**
- **¾ cup chopped green sweet pepper (1 medium)**
- **⅓ cup finely chopped onion (1 small)**
- **2 tablespoons brown sugar**
- **2 teaspoons mustard seed**
- **½ teaspoon ground cinnamon**
- **¼ teaspoon ground cloves**
- **⅛ teaspoon black pepper**
- **⅓ cup vinegar**
- **¼ cup water**
- **2 tablespoons catsup**

1. In a 4- or 6-quart pressure cooker combine the carrots, sweet pepper, onion, brown sugar, mustard seed, cinnamon, cloves, black pepper, vinegar, water, and catsup.

2. Lock lid in place. Place pressure regulator on vent pipe (if you have a first-generation cooker). Over high heat, bring cooker up to pressure. Reduce heat just enough to maintain pressure and pressure regulator rocks gently; cook for 2 minutes.

3. Quick-release the pressure. Carefully remove lid. Cool slightly; cover and refrigerate. Serve chilled. Makes 6 side-dish servings (3 cups).

Nutrition facts per serving: 65 calories, 1 g total fat (0 g saturated fat), 0 mg cholesterol, 116 mg sodium, 16 g carbohydrate, 3 g fiber, 1 g protein
Daily Value: 171% vitamin A, 20% vitamin C, 3% calcium, 6% iron

BEETS IN RUBY SAUCE

Sliced or cubed beets usually take 20 to 30 minutes to cook when simmered on the range top.
With this recipe you can enjoy tender beets in a sweet-sour cranberry-orange sauce in less than half the time.

PREPARATION TIME: 15 MINUTES
COOKING TIME: 7 MINUTES

4 **cups beets, peeled and
    cut into ½-inch cubes
    (8 medium)**
2 **tablespoons sugar**
1 **teaspoon grated orange
    peel**
¼ **teaspoon salt**
1½ **cups cranberry juice
    cocktail**
2 **tablespoons cornstarch**
2 **tablespoons water**

Select beets that are well
shaped, firm, small to
medium in size, and with a
healthy color and smooth
skin. Avoid very large beets,
as they may be tough, pithy,
and less sweet. Leaves
should be deep green and
fresh looking.

1. In a 4- or 6-quart pressure cooker combine the beets, sugar, orange peel, salt, and cranberry juice cocktail.

2. Lock lid in place. Place pressure regulator on vent pipe (if you have a first-generation cooker). Over high heat, bring cooker up to pressure. Reduce heat just enough to maintain pressure and pressure regulator rocks gently; cook for 3 minutes.

3. Quick-release the pressure. Carefully remove lid.

4. Stir together cornstarch and water till blended. Stir cornstarch mixture into the beet mixture in the pressure cooker. Cook and stir over medium heat till thickened and bubbly. Cook and stir for 2 minutes more. Makes 5 side-dish servings (3½ cups).

Nutrition facts per serving: *114 calories, 0 g total fat (0 g saturated fat), 0 mg cholesterol, 173 mg sodium, 27 g carbohydrate, 5 g fiber, 1 g protein*
Daily Value: *0% vitamin A, 57% vitamin C, 1% calcium, 6% iron*

GREEN BEANS WITH ORIENTAL SAUCE

Crisp-tender green beans, bits of red sweet pepper, and crunchy toasted walnuts are served in a light sauce scented with fresh ginger and garlic—an excellent accompaniment for grilled fish, poultry, or meat.

PREPARATION TIME: 20 MINUTES
COOKING TIME: 5 MINUTES

- 1 **tablespoon cooking oil**
- ½ **cup chopped walnuts**
- 6 **cups green beans, trimmed (1 pound)**
- 1 **clove garlic, minced**
- ½ **teaspoon minced gingerroot**
- ⅔ **cup vegetable broth or vegetable stock (page 35), chicken broth or chicken stock (page 36)**
- 2 **teaspoons cornstarch**
- 1 **teaspoon sugar**
- 1 **tablespoon water**
- ½ **cup diced red sweet pepper**
- ¼ **cup sliced green onions (2)**

1. In a 4- or 6-quart pressure cooker heat 1 tablespoon of the oil over medium heat. Cook the walnuts till they are toasted. With a slotted spoon remove the walnuts and drain on a paper towel.

2. Place beans, garlic, gingerroot, and vegetable or chicken broth or stock in the cooker.

3. Lock lid in place. Place pressure regulator on vent pipe (if you have a first-generation cooker). Over high heat, bring cooker up to pressure and cook till pressure regulator begins to rock slowly.

4. Quick-release the pressure. Carefully remove lid. With a slotted spoon remove the beans and keep warm.

5. Stir together the cornstarch, sugar, and water till blended. Stir the cornstarch mixture into the cooking liquid in the pressure cooker. Add the sweet pepper and green onions. Cook and stir over medium heat till thickened and bubbly. Stir in the beans and walnuts. Heat through. Makes 6 side-dish servings (4 cups).

Nutrition facts per serving: 120 calories, 9 g total fat (1 g saturated fat), 0 mg cholesterol, 210 mg sodium, 11 g carbohydrate, 3 g fiber, 3 g protein
Daily Value: 12% vitamin A, 37% vitamin C, 3% calcium, 8% iron

BRUSSELS SPROUTS IN GARLIC-CHEESE SAUCE

Brussels sprouts are miniature members of the cabbage family prized for their sweet mild flavor.
Cook the sprouts as soon as possible after harvesting or purchasing as they develop a strong flavor when stored.

PREPARATION TIME: 15 MINUTES
COOKING TIME: 6 MINUTES

- 4 **cups brussels sprouts, trimmed (about 1 pound)**
- 3 **cloves garlic, minced**
- ½ **teaspoon salt**
- ¼ **teaspoon dry mustard**
- ¼ **teaspoon black pepper**
- ⅔ **cup chicken broth or chicken stock (page 36)**
- 1 **tablespoon margarine or butter**
- 1 **tablespoon all-purpose flour**
- ½ **cup milk**
- 1 **cup shredded sharp cheddar cheese (4 ounces)**
  Paprika (optional)

1. In a 4- or 6-quart pressure cooker combine the brussels sprouts, garlic, salt, mustard, black pepper, chicken broth or stock, and margarine.

2. Lock lid in place. Place pressure regulator on vent pipe (if you have a first-generation cooker). Over high heat, bring cooker up to pressure. Reduce heat just enough to maintain pressure and pressure regulator rocks gently; cook for 1½ minutes.

3. Quick-release the pressure. Carefully remove lid. With a slotted spoon remove sprouts to a serving bowl and keep warm. Reserve ½ cup of the cooking liquid. Discard remaining cooking liquid.

4. In a small bowl, whisk together the flour and milk till smooth. Stir the milk mixture into the reserved liquid in the pressure cooker. Cook and stir over medium heat till thickened and bubbly. Cook and stir for 1 minute more.

5. Add the shredded cheese and stir till melted. Pour the sauce over the brussels sprouts. Sprinkle with paprika, if desired. Serve immediately. Makes 6 side-dish servings.

Nutrition facts per serving: 147 calories, 9 g total fat (5 g saturated fat), 22 mg cholesterol, 431 mg sodium, 10 g carbohydrate, 3 g fiber, 8 g protein
Daily Value: 15% vitamin A, 86% vitamin C, 16% calcium, 8% iron

BRAISED COLLARD GREENS WITH BACON AND CREAM

These mild-flavored greens are done to perfection in the pressure cooker just as soon as the pressure is reached. Be sure to quick-release the pressure immediately to avoid overcooking.

PREPARATION TIME: 20 MINUTES
COOKING TIME: 10 MINUTES

2 slices bacon, diced
⅓ cup chopped onion (1 small)
⅛ teaspoon black pepper
Dash ground nutmeg
¼ cup water
12 cups packed collard greens, stemmed and cut into 1-inch slices (1½ pounds)
¼ cup whipping cream

Collard greens are leafy vegetables that are a type of kale. The green leaves have an irregular shape and torn-looking edges. Collard greens have a hearty spinachlike flavor when cooked and are particularly popular in southern cooking.

1. In a 6-quart* pressure cooker cook the bacon till crisp over medium heat. With a slotted spoon remove the bacon and drain on paper towels. Set aside.

2. Stir the onion, black pepper, nutmeg, and water into the drippings in the pressure cooker. Add the collard greens.

3. Lock lid in place. Place pressure regulator on vent pipe (if you have a first-generation cooker). Over high heat, bring cooker up to pressure, cook till pressure regulator begins to rock slowly.

4. Quick-release the pressure. Carefully remove lid. Drain off liquid. Stir in the cream and cooked bacon. Makes 6 side-dish servings (4 cups).

*Note: If using a 4-quart pressure cooker, halve the recipe.

Nutrition facts per serving: 74 calories, 5 g total fat (3 g saturated fat), 15 mg cholesterol, 52 mg sodium, 7 g carbohydrate, 2 g fiber, 2 g protein
Daily Value: 27% vitamin A, 19% vitamin C, 2% calcium, 1% iron

Sweet and Sour Red Cabbage

*Serve this deliciously easy side dish of red cabbage, tart apples, onion, brown sugar,
and vinegar with stuffed pork chops or German-style pot roast (sauerbraten).*

Preparation Time: 15 minutes
Cooking Time: 0 minutes

6 **cups shredded red
cabbage**
1½ **cups chopped, peeled
tart apples (2 medium)**
½ **cup chopped onion
(1 medium)**
3 **tablespoons brown sugar**
¼ **teaspoon salt**
⅛ **teaspoon black pepper**
¼ **cup vinegar**
1 **tablespoon margarine or
butter**

1. In a 4- or 6-quart pressure cooker combine the cabbage, apples, onion, brown sugar, salt, black pepper, vinegar, and margarine.

2. Lock lid in place. Place pressure regulator on vent pipe (if you have a first-generation cooker). Over high heat, bring cooker up to pressure, cook till pressure regulator begins to rock slowly.

3. Quick-release pressure. Carefully remove lid. Makes 6 side-dish servings (3½ cups).

Nutrition facts per serving: *88 calories, 2 g total fat (0 g saturated fat), 0 mg cholesterol,
121 mg sodium, 18 g carbohydrate, 2 g fiber, 1 g protein*
Daily Value: *2% vitamin A, 70% vitamin C, 3% calcium, 4% iron*

COLCANNON

Potatoes, leeks, and cabbage or kale are cooked, then whipped together with milk and butter in this traditional Irish dish. Enjoy it with smoked ham or corned beef.

PREPARATION TIME: 15 MINUTES
COOKING TIME: 5 MINUTES

3 **cups coarsely chopped cabbage**
¾ **cup thinly sliced leeks, white part only (2 medium), or sliced green onions (6)**
⅔ **cup milk**
2 **tablespoons margarine or butter**
3 **cups potatoes, peeled and cut into ¼-inch slices (4 medium)**
½ **teaspoon salt**
⅛ **teaspoon black pepper**

A member of the onion family, leeks resemble an oversize green onion with overlapping wide green leaves, a flat white stalk, and shaggy roots at the bulb end. Leeks have a subtle onion flavor.

1. In a 4- or 6-quart pressure cooker place the cabbage, leeks, milk, and margarine or butter. Layer the potatoes over the cabbage mixture and sprinkle with salt and black pepper.

2. Lock lid in place. Place pressure regulator on vent pipe (if you have a first-generation cooker). Over high heat, bring cooker up to pressure. Reduce heat just enough to maintain pressure and pressure regulator rocks gently; cook for 5 minutes.

3. Quick-release the pressure. Carefully remove lid. (Vegetable mixture will appear curdled.)

4. Remove vegetable mixture to a large mixing bowl. Mash with a potato masher or with an electric mixer at low speed, adding additional milk, if necessary, to make light and fluffy. Makes 4 side-dish servings (2¾ cups).

Nutrition facts per serving: 246 calories, 7 g total fat (2 g saturated fat), 3 mg cholesterol, 385 mg sodium, 43 g carbohydrate, 4 g fiber, 6 g protein
Daily Value: 11% vitamin A, 83% vitamin C, 11% calcium, 14% iron

SWEET AND SOUR RED ONION RINGS

Savor these piquant onion rings with grilled meats and roasts, or chill and use them as sandwich toppers.
For a zesty vegetable combination, toss with crisp-tender steamed green beans.

PREPARATION TIME: 10 MINUTES
COOKING TIME: 0 MINUTES

4½ **cups red onions, cut into ¾-inch slices (3 large)**
¼   **teaspoon salt**
½   **cup water**
1   **tablespoon sugar**
⅛   **teaspoon black pepper**
3   **tablespoons balsamic vinegar**
1   **tablespoon margarine or butter**
1   **tablespoon snipped fresh parsley**

Select firm onions that have short necks and papery outer skins, and are free of blemishes and soft spots.

1. In a 4- or 6-quart pressure cooker combine the onions, salt, and water.

2. Lock lid in place. Place pressure regulator on vent pipe (if you have a first-generation cooker). Over high heat, bring cooker up to pressure. Reduce heat just enough to maintain pressure and pressure regulator rocks gently; cook for 2 minutes.

3. Quick-release the pressure. Carefully remove lid. Drain onions. Return onions to pressure cooker.

4. Add the sugar, black pepper, vinegar, and margarine or butter. Bring to boiling; reduce heat. Cook, stirring constantly, till the vinegar has evaporated and the onions are glazed, for 5 to 7 minutes. Sprinkle with parsley. Makes 6 side-dish servings (2½ cups).

Nutrition facts per serving: *75 calories, 2 g total fat (0 g saturated fat), 0 mg cholesterol, 116 mg sodium, 14 g carbohydrate, 2 g fiber, 1 g protein*
Daily Value: *2% vitamin A, 11% vitamin C, 1% calcium, 3% iron*

ORANGE-CANDIED PUMPKIN

Instead of candied sweet potatoes, enjoy pieces of pumpkin or winter squash cooked in a brown-sugar sauce delicately flavored with orange and spice.

PREPARATION TIME: 25 MINUTES
COOKING TIME: 2 MINUTES

- 1 **3½ inch stick cinnamon, broken up**
- 10 **whole cloves**
- ½ **teaspoon whole allspice**
- 1 **cup packed brown sugar**
- 1 **medium unpeeled orange, sliced and seeded**
- ½ **cup orange juice**
- ½ **cup water**
- 6 **cups pumpkin, buttercup or butternut squash, seeded, peeled and cut into 1-inch cubes (about 3 pounds)**
- 2 **tablespoons chopped walnuts, toasted**

1. For spice bag, tie the cinnamon, cloves, and allspice in a small piece of cheesecloth.

2. In a 4- or 6-quart pressure cooker combine the brown sugar, orange slices, orange juice, water, and spice bag. Add the pumpkin or squash.

3. Lock lid in place. Place pressure regulator on vent pipe (if you have a first-generation cooker). Over high heat, bring cooker up to pressure. Reduce heat just enough to maintain pressure and pressure regulator rocks gently; cook for 2 minutes.

4. Quick-release the pressure. Carefully remove lid.

5. With a slotted spoon remove the pumpkin to a large bowl. Discard the spice bag and orange slices. Drizzle ¼ cup of the cooking liquid over the pumpkin and sprinkle with nuts. Serve immediately. Makes 8 side-dish servings (5 cups).

Nutrition facts per serving: 157 calories, 1 g total fat (0 g saturated fat), 0 mg cholesterol, 12 mg sodium, 38 g carbohydrate, 3 g fiber, 2 g protein
Daily Value: 83% vitamin A, 57% vitamin C, 6% calcium, 8% iron

APPLE-STUFFED ACORN SQUASH

Plump raisins and tender pieces of apple spiced with cinnamon, nutmeg, and cloves make a savory filling for winter squash. The pressure cooker cooks this side dish in minutes compared to an hour in the oven.

PREPARATION TIME: 15 MINUTES
COOKING TIME: 6 MINUTES

¼ **cup packed brown sugar**
¼ **teaspoon ground cinnamon**
Dash ground nutmeg
Dash ground cloves
¾ **cup chopped, peeled tart apple (1 medium)**
2 **tablespoons raisins**
1 **1¼- to 1½-pound acorn squash, quartered lengthwise and seeded**
1 **tablespoon butter or margarine**
1 **cup water**

Choose an acorn squash with a deeply furrowed shell. It may be deep green, gold, or white with bright orange to off-white meat. An acorn squash can be stored in a cool dry place for up to 2 months.

1. In a medium bowl combine the brown sugar, cinnamon, nutmeg, and cloves. Stir in the apple and raisins. Dot squash quarters with butter. Spoon the apple mixture into the squash quarters.

2. Place rack in a 4-or 6-quart pressure cooker and add the water. Place the stuffed squash quarters on the rack, overlapping ends as necessary.

3. Lock lid in place. Place pressure regulator on vent pipe (if you have a first-generation cooker). Over high heat, bring cooker up to pressure. Reduce heat just enough to maintain pressure and pressure regulator rocks gently; cook for 6 minutes.

4. Quick-release the pressure and carefully remove the lid. Makes 4 side-dish servings.

Nutrition facts per serving: *147 calories, 3 g total fat (2 g saturated fat), 8 mg cholesterol, 38 mg sodium, 32 g carbohydrate, 3 g fiber, 1 g protein*
Daily Value: *86% vitamin A, 32% vitamin C, 5% calcium, 7% iron*

CARAMEL CUSTARD

*If using a metal ring mold for this recipe, protect your
hands with hot pads when coating the mold with the hot golden-sugar syrup.*

PREPARATION TIME: 20 MINUTES
COOKING TIME: 4 ½ MINUTES

⅓ **cup sugar**
3 **eggs**
⅓ **cup sugar**
1 **teaspoon vanilla**
1½ **cups half-and-half, light
cream, or milk**
1 **cup water**

1. In a heavy saucepan cook ⅓ cup sugar over medium-high heat (do not stir) till sugar begins to melt, shaking pan occasionally. Reduce heat to low and cook till sugar is golden, stirring frequently. Divide sugar mixture among four 6-ounce custard cups or pour into a 3-cup metal ring mold. Lift and tilt to coat bottom(s) and partway up sides. Set aside.

2. In a bowl combine eggs, ⅓ cup sugar, vanilla, and half-and-half. Beat till combined with whisk or rotary beater. Divide custard among prepared custard cups or pour into mold. Cover with foil. (If using the ring mold, punch hole in center of foil and fold foil down into center for easier lifting of ring mold.)

3. Place rack and water in a 4- or 6-quart pressure cooker. Place custard cups or ring mold on rack in cooker. (Depending on size of cooker, cook 2 to 4 custard cups at a time.)

4. Lock lid in place. Place pressure regulator on vent pipe (if you have a first-generation cooker). Over high heat, bring cooker up to pressure. Reduce heat just enough to maintain pressure and pressure regulator rocks gently; cook for 4½ minutes.

5. Quick-release the pressure. Carefully remove lid. Remove custard cups or ring mold. Remove foil and cool on wire rack. Cover and chill at least 4 hours. If desired, loosen edges of custard cups or ring mold with a spatula or knife; invert onto dessert plate(s). Makes 4 servings.

Nutrition facts per serving: *307 calories, 14 g total fat (8 g saturated fat), 193 mg cholesterol, 85 mg sodium, 38 g carbohydrate, 0 g fiber, 7 g protein*
Daily Value: *18% vitamin A, 1% vitamin C, 9% calcium, 4% iron*

VANILLA CUSTARD WITH RASPBERRIES

*This simply delicious creamy custard is as delightful made
with blueberries, blackberries, or thinly sliced peaches.*

PREPARATION TIME: 6 MINUTES
COOKING TIME: 2 MINUTES

¼ **cup fresh or frozen
   raspberries, thawed**
2 **beaten eggs**
3 **tablespoons sugar**
1 **cup milk**
1 **teaspoon vanilla**
⅛ **teaspoon ground nutmeg**
1 **cup water**
   **Fresh or frozen
   raspberries, thawed
   (optional)**

1. Divide raspberries among four 6-ounce custard cups or place in a
1-quart soufflé dish. (If using soufflé dish, tear off two 20x2-inch pieces
of heavy foil. Crisscross the strips and place dish in the center.) Set aside.

2. In a bowl combine eggs, sugar, milk, vanilla, and nutmeg. Beat till
smooth with whisk or rotary beater. Divide custard among prepared
custard cups or pour into soufflé dish. Cover each with foil.

3. Place rack and water in a 4- or 6-quart pressure cooker. Place custard
cups on a rack in cooker. Depending on size of cooker, cook
2 custard cups at a time, if necessary. (If using soufflé dish, bring up the
foil strips and lift the ends of the strips and transfer the dish into the
cooker. Fold ends of foil strips over the top of the dish.)

4. Lock lid in place. Place pressure regulator on vent pipe (if you have a
first-generation cooker). Over high heat, bring cooker up to pressure.
Reduce heat just enough to maintain pressure and pressure regulator
rocks gently; cook for 2 minutes.

5. Quick-release the pressure. Carefully remove lid.

6. Carefully remove custard cups from cooker. (If using soufflé dish, use
foil strips to carefully lift the soufflé dish out of the cooker.) Remove foil.
Serve warm or chilled. If desired, unmold chilled custard cups and
garnish with additional raspberries. Makes 4 servings.

Nutrition facts per serving: *112 calories, 4 g total fat (2 g saturated fat), 111 mg cholesterol,
62 mg sodium, 14 g carbohydrate, 0 g fiber, 5 g protein*
Daily Value: *8% vitamin A, 4% vitamin C, 7% calcium, 2% iron*

PEAR CHERRY COMPOTE

For an added touch, sprinkle compote with cookie or graham cracker crumbs.

PREPARATION TIME: 15 MINUTES
COOKING TIME: 30 SECONDS

· · · · · · ·

- 1 **lemon**
- 2 **pounds pears, peeled, cored, and cut into lengthwise quarters**
- ½ **cup dried tart cherries or dried cranberries**
- ½ **cup sugar**
- ½ **cup orange juice**
- 3 **inches stick cinnamon**
- 6 **whole cloves**

The best way to ripen pears is to place the firm pears in a paper bag or a loosely covered bowl. Let them stand at room temperature for a few days. You can tell most varieties are ripe when they yield to gentle pressure at the stem end. Once ripened, you can keep fresh pears in the refrigerator for several days.

1. Using a vegetable peeler, remove thin strips of peel from lemon. Save lemon for another use.

2. In a 4- or 6-quart pressure cooker combine lemon peel, pears, cherries or cranberries, sugar, orange juice, cinnamon, and cloves.

3. Lock lid in place. Place pressure regulator on vent pipe (if you have a first-generation cooker). Over high heat, bring cooker up to pressure. Reduce heat just enough to maintain pressure and pressure regulator rocks gently; cook for 30 seconds.

4. Quick-release the pressure. Carefully remove lid. Transfer to nonmetal bowl. Cover and chill till serving time. Remove cinnamon and cloves before serving. Makes 6 servings (3 cups).

Nutrition facts per serving: 197 calories, 1 g total fat (0 g saturated fat), 0 mg cholesterol, 0 mg sodium, 50 g carbohydrate, 5 g fiber, 1 g protein
Daily Value: 67% vitamin A, 28% vitamin C, 1% calcium, 2% iron

CINNAMON RICOTTA CHEESECAKE

*You can sweeten the fresh fruit mix with a little sugar
or honey before spooning it over the cheesecake.*

PREPARATION TIME: 15 MINUTES
COOKING TIME: 10 MINUTES

- ¾ **cup ricotta cheese**
- ½ **of a 3-ounce package cream cheese**
- ½ **cup sugar**
- 2 **eggs**
- 2 **tablespoons dairy sour cream or plain yogurt**
- 1 **tablespoon all-purpose flour**
- ½ **teaspoon ground cinnamon**
- 1 **cup water**
  Whipped cream (optional)
  Assorted cut-up fruit such as sliced peaches, halved strawberries, or sliced kiwi, (optional)

1. Grease four 6-ounce custard cups. Set aside.

2. In blender container or food processor bowl, place ricotta, cream cheese, sugar, eggs, sour cream or yogurt, flour, and cinnamon. Cover and blend or process till smooth. Pour into prepared cups and cover each with foil.

3. Place rack and water in a 4- or 6-quart pressure cooker. Place 2 to 4 cups on rack.

4. Lock lid in place. Place pressure regulator on vent pipe (if you have a first-generation cooker). Over high heat, bring cooker up to pressure. Reduce heat just enough to maintain pressure and pressure regulator rocks gently; cook for 10 minutes.

5. Quick-release the pressure. Carefully remove lid.

6. Carefully remove custard cups from cooker. Remove foil. Place on a wire rack and cool to room temperature. Cover and chill for 2 to 24 hours. If desired, run a knife around edge of custard cups and unmold onto dessert plates. Serve with whipped cream and fresh fruit, if desired. Makes 4 servings.

Nutrition facts per serving: *258 calories, 11 g total fat (6 g saturated fat), 136 mg cholesterol, 125 mg sodium, 30 g carbohydrate, 0 g fiber, 10 g protein*
Daily Value: *17% vitamin A, 0% vitamin C, 13% calcium, 6% iron*

CREAMY CHOCOLATE CHEESECAKE

Use your microwave to speed up preparation time for this dessert.
Just microwave the cream cheese for 1 minute on high setting and stir till smooth.

PREPARATION TIME: 15 MINUTES
COOKING TIME: 3 ½ MINUTES
(6-OUNCE CUSTARD CUPS)
25 TO 30 MINUTES (SPRINGFORM PAN)

¼ **cup chocolate graham cracker crumbs, graham cracker crumbs, or chocolate wafer crumbs**

12 **ounces cream cheese, softened**

½ **cup sugar**

1 **tablespoon all-purpose flour**

3 **eggs**

1 **teaspoon vanilla**

4 **ounces semisweet chocolate, melted and cooled**

2 **cups water**
Sweetened whipped cream (optional)
Shaved chocolate (optional)

1. Grease a 6- or 7-inch springform pan on sides and bottom. Coat bottom of pan with crumbs. Set aside. Tear off two 20x2-inch pieces of heavy foil. Crisscross the strips and place pan in the center.

2. In blender container or food processor bowl place cream cheese, sugar, flour, eggs, and vanilla. Cover and blend or process till smooth. Add melted chocolate. Cover and blend or process till smooth. Pour into prepared pan and cover with foil.

3. Place rack and water in a 4- or 6-quart pressure cooker. Bringing up the foil strips, lift the ends of the strips and transfer pan into the cooker. Fold ends of foil strips over the top of the pan.

4. Lock lid in place. Place the pressure regulator on the vent pipe (if you have a first-generation cooker). Over high heat, bring cooker up to pressure. Reduce the heat just enough to maintain pressure and pressure regulator rocks gently; cook for 30 minutes for the 6-inch pan or 25 minutes for the 7-inch pan.

5. Allow pressure to come down naturally. Carefully remove lid.

6. Using foil strips, carefully lift cheesecake out of the cooker. Remove foil. Place on a wire rack and cool 15 minutes; loosen sides of cheesecake. Cool to room temperature. Remove sides of pan. Cover and chill for 2 to 24 hours. Garnish with whipped cream and shaved chocolate, if desired. Makes 8 servings.

Nutrition facts per serving: 311 calories, 22 g total fat (13 g saturated fat), 127 mg cholesterol, 166 mg sodium, 25 g carbohydrate, 1 g fiber, 7 g protein
Daily Value: 21% vitamin A, 0% vitamin C, 4% calcium, 9% iron

WHOLE WHEAT CINNAMON-RAISIN BREAD PUDDING

Bread puddings are a great way to have dessert in minutes for those unexpected guests.

PREPARATION TIME: 12 MINUTES
COOK TIME: 20 MINUTES

- 4 **beaten eggs**
- 2 **cups milk**
- ¼ **cup granulated sugar**
- ¼ **cup packed brown sugar**
- 1 **teaspoon vanilla**
- ½ **teaspoon ground cinnamon**
- 3 **cups whole wheat bread cubes (4 slices)**
- ⅓ **cup raisins**
- 1 **cup water**

1. Grease an 1½-quart soufflé dish. Tear off two 20x2-inch pieces of heavy foil. Crisscross the strips and place dish in the center.

2. In a mixing bowl beat together the eggs, milk, granulated sugar, brown sugar, vanilla, and cinnamon using a wire whisk or rotary beater. Add bread cubes and raisins. Let stand 5 minutes.

3. Place rack and water in a 4- or 6-quart pressure cooker. Pour bread mixture into prepared soufflé dish and cover with foil. Bringing up the foil strips, lift the ends of the strips and transfer dish into the cooker. Fold ends of foil strips over the top of the dish.

4. Lock lid in place. Place pressure regulator on vent pipe (if you have a first-generation cooker). Over high heat, bring cooker up to pressure. Reduce heat just enough to maintain pressure and pressure regulator rocks gently; cook for 20 minutes.

5. Allow pressure to come down naturally. Carefully remove lid.

6. Using foil strips, carefully lift bread pudding out of the cooker. Remove foil. Place on a wire rack and cool 15 minutes. Serve warm or cover and chill. Makes 6 servings.

Nutrition facts per serving: *223 calories, 6 g total fat (2 g saturated fat), 148 mg cholesterol, 205 mg sodium, 35 g carbohydrate, 2 g fiber, 9 g protein*
Daily Value: *11% vitamin A, 1% vitamin C, 11% calcium, 10% iron*

CRANBERRY BREAD PUDDING

*Perfect for a casual holiday gathering, this comforting dessert will be
the center of conversation with its rich and flavorful bourbon sauce.*

PREPARATION TIME: 15 MINUTES
COOK TIME: 25 MINUTES

- **4 beaten eggs**
- **2 cups milk**
- **½ cup granulated sugar**
- **1 teaspoon vanilla**
- **3 cups dry bread cubes
  (see tip page 93)**
- **⅓ cup dried cranberries,
  dried cherries, or
  raisins**
- **1½ cups water
  Bourbon Sauce or
  whipped cream
  (optional)**
- **⅓ cup chopped pecans or
  walnuts (optional)**

1. Grease a 1½-quart soufflé dish. Tear off two 20x2-inch pieces of heavy foil. Crisscross the strips and place dish in the center.

2. In a bowl beat together the eggs, milk, sugar, and vanilla using a wire whisk. Place bread cubes and dried cranberries in prepared dish. Pour egg mixture over bread mixture and cover with foil.

3. Place rack and water in a 4- or 6-quart pressure cooker. Bringing up the foil strips, lift the ends of the strips and transfer dish into the cooker. Fold ends of foil strips over the top of the dish.

4. Lock lid in place. Place pressure regulator on vent pipe. Over high heat, bring cooker up to pressure. Reduce heat just enough to maintain pressure and pressure regulator rocks gently; cook for 25 minutes.

5. Allow pressure to come down naturally. Carefully remove lid.

6. Using foil strips, lift bread pudding out of the cooker. Remove foil. Place on a wire rack and cool 15 minutes. Serve warm or cover and chill. If desired, serve with Bourbon Sauce or whipped cream and sprinkle with nuts. Makes 6 servings.

BOURBON SAUCE: In a saucepan melt ¼ cup *margarine or butter.* Remove from heat and stir in ½ cup *sugar.* Stir together 1 beaten *egg yolk* and 2 tablespoons *water.* Add to sugar mixture, stirring constantly. Cook and stir over medium-low heat for 4 to 5 minutes or till sugar dissolves and mixture just begins to bubble. Remove from heat. Stir in 2 tablespoons *bourbon.* Serve warm. Makes about ¾ cup.

Nutrition facts per serving: 227 calories, 6 g total fat (2 g saturated fat), 148 mg cholesterol, 186 mg sodium, 36 g carbohydrate, 0 g fiber, 9 g protein
Daily Value: 11% vitamin A, 1% vitamin C, 11% calcium, 7% iron

CHOCOLATE-CINNAMON BREAD PUDDING

Chocolate lovers will applaud this old-fashioned favorite
especially if you serve it with a pour of hot fudge sauce.

PREPARATION TIME: 10 MINUTES
COOK TIME: 30 MINUTES

4 beaten eggs
2 cups milk
¼ cup granulated sugar
1 teaspoon vanilla
½ teaspoon ground
   cinnamon
3 cups dry bread cubes
   (see tip below)
1 6-ounce package
   semisweet chocolate
   pieces
   (1 cup)
2 cups water

To dry bread cubes, start with about 3½ cups (4½ slices). Spread in a single layer in a shallow baking pan. Bake in a 300° oven for 10 to 15 minutes or till dry, stirring twice. Or, let stand, loosely covered, at room temperature for 8 to 12 hours. Measure 3 cups.

1. Grease a 1½-quart soufflé dish. Tear off two 20x2-inch pieces of heavy foil. Crisscross the strips and place dish in the center.

2. In a mixing bowl beat together the eggs, milk, sugar, vanilla, and cinnamon using a wire whisk or rotary beater. Place bread cubes and chocolate in prepared dish. Pour egg mixture over bread mixture and cover with foil.

3. Place rack and water in a 4- or 6-quart pressure cooker. Bringing up the foil strips, lift the ends of the strips and transfer dish into the cooker. Fold ends of foil strips over the top of the dish.

4. Lock lid in place. Place pressure regulator on vent pipe (if you have a first-generation cooker). Over high heat, bring cooker up to pressure. Reduce heat just enough to maintain pressure and pressure regulator rocks gently; cook for 30 minutes.

5. Allow pressure to come down naturally. Carefully remove lid.

6. Using foil strips, carefully lift bread pudding out of the cooker. Remove foil. Place on a wire rack and cool 15 minutes. Serve warm. Makes 6 servings.

Nutrition facts per serving: *304 calories, 14 g total fat (2 g saturated fat), 148 mg cholesterol, 173 mg sodium, 40 g carbohydrate, 0 g fiber, 10 g protein*
Daily Value: *11% vitamin A, 1% vitamin C, 12% calcium, 12% iron*

PEAR BREAD PUDDING

Delicious as is or top with a spoon of sweetened whipped cream or a flavored fruit yogurt.

PREPARATION TIME: 18 MINUTES
COOK TIME: 20 MINUTES

- 4 **beaten eggs**
- 2 **cups milk**
- ¼ **cup granulated sugar**
- ¼ **cup packed brown sugar**
- 1 **teaspoon vanilla**
- ½ **teaspoon ground nutmeg**
- ½ **teaspoon ground ginger**
- 3 **cups dry whole wheat bread cubes (see tip page 93)**
- ⅓ **cup cut-up dried pears, apricots, or apples**
- 1 **cup water**

1. Grease a 1½-quart soufflé dish. Tear off two 20x2-inch pieces of heavy foil. Crisscross the strips and place dish in the center.

2. In a mixing bowl beat together the eggs, milk, granulated sugar, brown sugar, vanilla, nutmeg, and ginger using a wire whisk or rotary beater. Place bread cubes and dried fruit in prepared dish. Pour egg mixture over bread mixture and cover with foil.

3. Place rack and water in a 4- or 6-quart pressure cooker. Bringing up the foil strips, lift the ends of the strips and transfer dish into the cooker. Fold ends of foil strips over the top of the dish.

4. Lock lid in place. Place pressure regulator on vent pipe (if you have a first-generation cooker). Over high heat, bring cooker up to pressure. Reduce heat just enough to maintain pressure and pressure regulator rocks gently; cook for 20 minutes.

5. Allow pressure to come down naturally. Carefully remove lid.

6. Using foil strips, carefully lift bread pudding out of the cooker. Remove foil. Place on a wire rack and cool 15 minutes. Serve warm or cover and chill. Makes 6 servings.

Nutrition facts per serving: *226 calories, 6 g total fat (2 g saturated fat), 148 mg cholesterol, 204 mg sodium, 36 g carbohydrate, 3 g fiber, 9 g protein*
Daily Value: *11% vitamin A, 2% vitamin C, 11% calcium, 10% iron*